The jm-education Guide to Higher Music

Joe McGowan

www.jm-education.com

Joe McGowan
Rosebank
Rutherglen
Glasgow

For information contact: www.jmeducationweb@gmail.com
Website: www.jm-education.com

Cover design & music examples by Joe McGowan for jm-education

ISBN: 9781654133986

Although every effort has been made to ensure that website addresses are correct at the time of going to press, jm-education cannot be held responsible for the content of any website mentioned in this book except www.jm-education.com. It is sometimes possible to find a relocated web page by typing the address of the home page for a website in the URL window of your browser.

Acknowledgements

With grateful thanks to the following:

Sharon O'Riordan, Eddie McVey (proof reader)

www.jm-education.com

Online music lessons & consultations

www.yourmusicmentor.com

Also by Joe McGowan:

'How to Pass National 5 Music'

Pub: Hodder Gibson

Available online & in selected bookstores

Resources in the jm-education music range

Available online from *jm-education* in all amazon marketplaces, including amazon.co.uk and amazon.com

Music Manuscript Paper 6 large staves per page

Music Manuscript Paper 10 staves per page

Music Manuscript Paper 12 staves per page

Music Manuscript Paper 14 staves per page

4-String Tab Paper (Bass, Ukulele, Mandolin etc.) 10 staves per page

5-String Tab Paper (Banjo, 5-string Bass etc.) 8 staves per page

6-String Tab Paper (Guitar, 6-string Banjo etc.) 8 staves per page

Piano Manuscript Paper with treble and bass clefs. 5 double staves per page

Treble Clef Manuscript Paper (large) with treble clef. 6 staves per page

Bass Clef Manuscript Paper (large) with bass clef. 6 staves per page

Treble Clef Manuscript Paper (standard) with treble clef. 10 staves per page

Bass Clef Manuscript Paper (standard) with bass clef. 10 staves per page

Songwriters' Manuscript Paper with lyrics line. 8 staves per page

Staff & 4-string Tab Paper (Bass, Ukulele, Mandolin etc.) 5 double staves per page

Staff & 5-string Tab Paper (Banjo, 5-string Bass etc.) 5 double staves per page

Staff & 6-string Tab Paper (Guitar, 6-string Banjo etc.) 5 double staves per page

4-String Chord Boxes and Fretboard Grids (blank) (Bass, Ukulele, Mandolin etc.)

5-String Chord Boxes and Fretboard Grids (blank) (Banjo, 5-string Bass etc.)

6-String Chord Boxes and Fretboard Grids (blank) (Guitar, 6-string Banjo etc.)

For new books by *jm-education* see amazon.com (or .uk) or jm-education.com

Contents

Introduction

Welcome to the jm-education Guide to Higher Music!

This book is a comprehensive overview of the Higher Music course with helpful exercises and expert advice that will prepare you for each area of assessment in Listening, Composing and Performing music. You will also get lots of extra little tips and guidelines along the way.

In addition, the book is supported with supplementary material and revision resources for both the Higher and National 5 music courses on the jm-education website (**www.jm-education.com**), including audio examples and exercises for every musical concept you need to know. So you can consider jm-education your new study partner!

Okay, then. Let's get started together...

The Higher Music Qualification

Note: More information can be obtained from the websites listed on page ix.

Higher Music gives you the opportunity to extend the knowledge and skills you acquired from previous musical study such as National 5 Music. As in this earlier grade, you will be involved in **Listening**, **Composing** and **Performing** music (and there is also a **Music Literacy** component), but you have a number of options within the Composing and Performing areas to cater for your personal musical interests and abilities.

Each of the main components to be assessed will be marked by an external assessor, but your teacher will guide and help to prepare you for each assignment. A total of **130 marks** are available, divided as shown in the table below.

Assessment marking structure table		
Component	Marks	Scaled mark
Listening Question paper (including Music Literacy)	40	35
Composing assignment	30	15
Performance (instrument 1)	30	25
Performance (instrument 2)	30	25
Total	130	100

Listening Question Paper
40 marks

See also chapters 1, 2 & 3. For possible updates to this area of the course check **www.sqa.org.uk**

Assessment:

- **Music question paper of one hour's duration (externally marked)**

During your course you will learn a range of new musical concepts which will be heard in practice and in a selection of musical works in various styles which you will study with your teacher.

In May of the exam year you will sit a one hour Listening question paper based on these concepts and Music Literacy (see chapter 3). **Note**: Candidates must also understand concepts from National 3, 4 and 5 music as this question paper will include some concepts from these earlier grades (see the *Glossary* for a list of all the relevant musical concepts).

Composing assignment
30 marks

See also chapter 4. For possible updates to this area of the course check **www.sqa.org.uk**

Assessment:

- **One piece of music lasting at least 1 minute and no more than 3 minutes 30 seconds composed by the candidate. (Conducted under teacher guidance and supervision and externally marked.) 20 marks.**

- **Composing review written by the candidate (externally marked). 10 marks.**

Candidates will plan and create a complete composition that contains at least three of these four elements: **melody**, **rhythm**, **structure**, **timbre**, and *must* also show use of **harmony**.

Upon completion of the work, the candidate should then write a review of the composition describing the compositional methods used and decisions taken as a result of exploring and developing various musical ideas. Strong areas of the composition should be identified, as well as those which could possibly be improved. (A sample composing review is given on page 87.)

Submission requirements:

- An audio recording of the composition

- A musical score or performing plan/diagram

- A written composing review (approximately 200-350 words in length)

Performing   60 marks

See chapter 5. For details and possible updates to this area of the course, check *www.sqa.org*

Assessment:

- **Performance instrument 1 (marked by a visiting assessor)** 30 marks

- **Performance instrument 2 (marked by a visiting assessor)** 30 marks

The performance can be solo and/or in a group setting. The overall programme length must be a **minimum** of **12 minutes** and **maximum 13 minutes**. The performance time on either of the two selected instruments, or instrument and voice, must be a **minimum** of **4 minutes** within the overall 12-13 minute programme.

Candidates should perform a minimum of **two** contrasting pieces of music on each of the two selected instruments, or instrument and voice. These should be of an appropriate standard/level of difficulty, which is **grade 4** or above (see Chapter 5, Performing).

The 60 marks available represent a scaled mark of 50% of the total mark. Each piece of music in the programme will be given a mark out of 10, but as the number of pieces in the programme is variable within the prescribed time restrictions, scaling will be used to determine the final mark.

How to use this book

The structure of this book makes it suitable for use both as a textbook during the Higher music course and as a revision guide when the final exams and assessments are approaching. You don't have to work through the book in any particular order, but, since most of the chapters require a good knowledge of musical concepts (including those from previous grades up to National 5), you may find it best to complete **Chapter 1**, **Musical Concepts**, before tackling other parts of the book.

Chapter content

Note: Audio material for chapters 1, 2, 3 and 4 can be accessed on the jm-education YouTube channel at *www.youtube/jm-education*. All of the musical concepts you need to understand appear in **bold** throughout the book.

Chapter 1 covers all the new musical concepts introduced at Higher level through a series of listening exercises in a similar format to the final Question Paper. The chapter is supported with revision tips and hints to help you recognise concepts when you hear them.

Chapter 2 provides information on the requirements for the Music Literacy component, including musical illustrations and two specimen listening exercises in a similar format to those featured in the final Question Paper.

Chapter 3 consists of a complete specimen listening Question Paper similar to the kind you will sit at the end of your Higher Music course.

Chapter 4 is a composing workshop in which you are guided step-by-step through the creative processes involved in composing a Scots Ballad with a melody line (to which words can be added) with piano accompaniment. In this chapter you have the opportunity to compose your own piece in a similar style, step-by-step, as you go through the workshop.

Chapter 5 provides an extensive range of practice and performance techniques for the Performing component of the Higher Music course, as well as information, tips and advice for the exam.

Glossary of musical concepts

Definitions of the musical concepts introduced in Higher Music can be found in the *Glossary* section on page 124. A list of the National 3-5 concepts which you also need to know is given on pages 130-131.

To help you as you work through the book

Bold concepts. Words appearing in **bold** throughout the book remind you that this word is a musical concept whose meaning you must fully understand.

www.jm-education.com is the companion website to this book. It contains free supplementary resource material for teacher and student use, including links to music concept examples and additional composing material with two full composing workshops and various other pieces of helpful information.

How to Pass National 5 Music. This book, also by Joe McGowan, contains all the material relating to National 5 Music that you need to understand before moving on to study Higher Music. The book can be purchased from bookstores, online via *amazon.co.uk* or the jm-education website shop, or directly from the publisher, Hodder Gibson *www.hoddereducation.co.uk* .

Exercises, notes, audio clips and top tips!

There are lots of targeted exercises, links to audio examples, important notes and little pieces of advice all through the book. These are presented in four main categories:

The purpose of these exercises is to present you with tasks and exercises which allow you to put into practice many of the techniques and concepts you will encounter through the book, as well as ensure that you understand the material you are working on.

Audio icon

 Listen in

A lot of the content in the book (exercises, musical examples etc.) is supported by videos and audio excerpts which can be accessed either by clicking the audio icons displayed on the *Listen in* exercises (if you are using an e-book), or accessing the jm-education YouTube channel at **www.youtube/jm-education**

 Take Note

These banners point out especially important information of which you should take note!

 **Top Tip**

Helpful little extra snippets of information are given throughout the book, including expert advice on ways to approach certain aspects of musical study that will make them a bit easier to undertake.

Online resources

The following online resources have material that will be extremely helpful as you work through this book. From advice and updates on your course to a wealth of additional resource material for both Higher and National 5 Music, these sites are companions that will give added power to your study and revision work.

Essential online resources		
Resource	**Description**	**Web address**
jm-education website	The jm-education website contains lots of supplementary material, resources, workshops and helpful links etc. for the Higher and National 5 Music courses.	**www.jm-education.com**
jm-education YouTube channel	The jm-education YouTube channel contains all of the audio material for this book, as well as Higher Music concept tutorial videos that will help you with chapters 1 and 3. There is also material for National 5 Music.	**www.youtube/jm-education**
Your Music Mentor	An online teaching service directed by Joe McGowan where students of Higher and National 5 Music can obtain private tuition	**www.yourmusicmentor.com**
The Scottish Qualifications Authority	Information, exam arrangements and updates on Scottish curriculum Music courses from National 3 to Advanced Higher	**www.sqa.org.uk**
The Associated Board of the Royal Schools of Music	Publications relating to graded ABRSM music exams (including free downloadable syllabuses with details of pieces for different instruments at each grade) and music theory.	**www.abrsm.org**
Trinity College London	Online music resources and publications relating to graded music exams (including free syllabuses with details of pieces for different instruments at each grade) and music theory.	**www.trinitycollege.com**
London College of Music	Online music resources and publications relating to graded music exams and music theory.	**www.uwl.ac.uk**
Rock School	Numerous publications relating to the study of rock and pop music and related instruments - including Rock School exam books for grades 1 - 8.	**www.rslawards.com**
Royal Conservatoire Scotland (RCS)	Information on graded exams in traditional music	**www.rcs.ac.uk**

Notes

Chapter 1 Musical Concepts

In this chapter you will revise all of the musical concepts you need to know for Higher Music, mainly through a series of listening-based exercises. To help you do this more effectively, the concepts have been divided into five separate units corresponding to their musical category.

- **Unit 1: STYLE** concepts

- **Unit 2: MELODY/HARMONY** concepts

- **Unit 3: RHYTHM/TEMPO** concepts

- **Unit 4: TEXTURE/STRUCTURE/FORM** concepts

- **Unit 5: TIMBRE/DYNAMICS** concepts

 **Take Note**

Targeting the concepts one category at a time will strengthen your understanding of them and your ability to recognise them by ear.

Before tackling the exercises, read through *Suggested revision strategies* below for helpful ideas on effective revision, and note that a tutorial video on each concept category is available to watch on the jm-education You Tube channel. The listening exercises also incorporate some concepts from National 5 Music which you should know, so don't forget to revise those as well!

The exercises

The audio material for the following units can be accessed on the Higher Music concept excerpt videos at ***www.youtube/jm-education*** or by clicking on the relevant audio icons (e-book).

Each unit is based on a series of listening questions in a similar format to that used in the Question Paper at the end of your course (see also Chapter 3). These exercises will therefore give you some additional practice for this final test question paper.

Suggested revision strategies

The following pages offer you some helpful revision advice before attempting the listening exercises in this chapter.

 Great advice... **Top Tip**

You can improve your ability to identify various musical **STYLES** by listening to an example of each (see page 4) and making a note of the unique or characteristic features as you listen. For example, **plainchant** has only male voices, often in **unison**, with **melismatic** singing and **modal** melodies; a **sonata** usually features **solo piano** (but perhaps **piano** and another instrument), and so on. Then, tune into a few radio stations, randomly listening to different types of music, and see if you can recognise the styles. This type of exercise can also be used for other concept categories in this chapter.

Revision strategy 1: Resources

Make use of the jm-education resources to do some preparatory work in the following order:

- **Review all National 5 Music concepts** as some of these also appear in this chapter's exercises. You will find a full list of what you need to know in the Glossary section (pages 130-131).

- **Watch the National 5 Music concept video examples** which are available to access on the *Resources* page of the jm-education website.

- **Refer to the book 'How to Pass National 5 Music'** (available from the *Shop* on the jm-education website, as well as larger bookstores and *amazon.co.uk*)

- **Watch the Higher Music concept tutorial videos** on the *Resources* page of the jm-education website, then try the listening exercises based on a particular category in this chapter (e.g. **STYLE** concepts). You may also like to watch the additional Higher Music concept video examples available on this *Resources* page.

Show a little style

Certain musical **STYLES** sometimes have features in common which might make it a little difficult to tell them apart by ear. The **Mass** and **Oratorio**, for example, are both vocal works which may present such a challenge.

One way to approach this identification problem is, rather than allow yourself to be distracted by the similarities, make sure you understand and can identify the features which separate one from the other. For instance, in an **Oratorio** you will be expecting to hear an **orchestra** and **choruses**, and perhaps also **soloists**, so the whole structure is generally 'bigger' and less 'solemn' than the **Mass** - which has clearly defined sections such as the **Kyrie**, **Gloria**, **Credo**, and **Sanctus Benedictus** (see Glossary, page 124). These Latin words are sung in the **Mass**, so if you hear the word '**Kyrie**' or '**Credo**' being sung then you are almost certainly listening to a **Mass**. Similarly, the absence of such key words would normally eliminate the possibility of the work being a **Mass**.

You can therefore often identify the **Style** of a piece of music not only by picking out what you hear but also by eliminating what you DO NOT hear.

 **Activity!**

Revision strategy 2: Brainstorm

Write down or discuss with your classmates what you know about the concepts from the categories in each unit (see individual units for concept lists) and consider whether you would be able to recognise each one by ear. Things to think about are: the main characteristic(s) of each concept and, where appropriate, the names of any particular songs/pieces you know which contain or represent a concept, together with their composer(s). Your descriptions needn't be too detailed; single words or brief explanations may be enough - whatever information helps you to identify the concept.

Below is an example of the kind of chart you could use for these *Brainstorm* exercises. A blank chart is available to download/print free from the *Resources* page on the jm-education website.

Listening Observation Chart		
Piece title	**Composer/ performer**	**Concepts present**
Minuetto from op.6, no.10	*A. Corelli*	*Basso continuo, concerto grosso, modulation, perfect cadence, trill, ripieno, concertino, Baroque*
Movement 3 from symphony 3	*Saint Saens*	*3 against 2, imitation, sequence, cymbals, Romantic, symphony*
Introduction and Allegro	*M. Ravel*	*Clarinet, pizzicato, sequence, harp, rubato, glissando, harmonics, Romantic*
Movement 3 from Concerto for orchestra	*P. Glass*	*Snare drum, triangle, timpani, violin, legato, concerto, minimalism*

 **Activity!**

Keep on listening

Listening to different kinds of music is the only way to become better at identifying concepts by ear. When you have worked through all of the units in this chapter, select recordings of music in a wide variety of musical styles and periods (from baroque to the present day) and listen carefully to identify as many concepts and features as you can in the different types of music.

Unit 1 STYLE Concepts

Higher Music STYLE concepts

● Sonata	● Plainchant	● Chamber music	● Jazz-funk
● Mass	● Oratorio	● Impressionist	● Soul music
● Recitative	● Musique concrète	● String quartet	● Lied

Instructions and guidance for the listening exercises in Unit 1

 Take Note

In this unit's exercises (questions 1 to 11) you will have to identify Higher Music **STYLE** concepts from the list above (no other Higher Music concepts will feature), together with general National 5 Music concepts.

Each question requires you to listen to a musical excerpt and provide answers in the spaces provided in pages 5-7. The questions are in the following format:

(a) requires a Higher Music STYLE concept ONLY for an answer.

(b) and (c) require a general National 5 Music concept for an answer.

Answers to the exercises in Unit 1 are given on page 132.

 Listen in

The musical excerpts for use with this unit are on the video, **'Higher Music concept excerpts for unit 1'**, which can be accessed by clicking on the audio icon above (e-book) or on the jm-education YouTube channel at **www.youtube/jm-education**.

- **Read through each question before listening to the music.**

- **Each excerpt will be played TWICE with a pause of 10 seconds between playings and a pause of 40 seconds before the next question starts.**

- **Complete your answers after hearing each excerpt no more than TWICE.**

Unit 1. STYLE concepts listening exercises   www.youtube.com/jm-education

Question 1

Higher Music concept: (a) Listen to this excerpt and identify the style of the music. _Soul_ ✓

National 5 concepts: (b) Listen to the excerpt again and describe the Time Signature. _Simple $\frac{3}{4}$_

(c) Name the keyboard instrument playing in the piece. _Synth ?? piano_

Question 2

Higher Music concept: (a) Listen to this excerpt and identify the style of the music. _Oratorio Mass_

National 5 concepts: (b) Listen to the excerpt again and describe the Time Signature. _$\frac{4}{4}$_ ✓

(c) Name a concept that describes a feature of the singing. _Melismatic_ ✓

Question 3

Higher Music concept: (a) Listen to this excerpt and identify the style of the music. _impressionist_ _Chamber Music_

National 5 concepts: (b) Listen to the excerpt again and write the Italian
word that describes the free or loose tempo. _rubato_ ✓

(c) Instruments from which family of the orchestra play the melody? _woodwind_

Question 4

Higher Music concept: (a) Listen to this excerpt and identify the style of the music. _Chamber_ _Impressionist_

National 5 concepts: (b) Listen to the excerpt again and name the **three** instruments playing.

Instrument 1. _piano_ ✓

Instrument 2. _violin_ ✓

Instrument 3. _viola? cello_

Question 5

Higher Music concept: (a) Listen to this excerpt and identify the style of the music. _recitative_ _oratorio_

National 5 concepts: (b) Listen to the excerpt again and describe the vocal range
(e.g. alto, mezzo-soprano etc.) of the female voice. _~~mezzo~~-soprano_

(c) Name the instrument that accompanies the singers. _harpsichord_ ✓

Question 6

Higher Music concept: (a) Listen to this excerpt and identify the style of the music. _Plainchant_

National 5 concepts: (b) Listen to the excerpt again and tick **two** boxes to describe features present

[✓] Homophonic   [ ] Backing vocals   [ ] Descant

[ ] Polyphonic   [✓] Melismatic   [ ] Round

Question 7

Higher Music concept: (a) Listen to this excerpt and identify the style of the music. _Sonata Impressionist_

National 5 concepts: (b) Listen to the excerpt again and tick **two** boxes to describe features present

[ ] Inverted pedal   [✓] Cluster chord   [ ] Vamp

[ ] Glissando   [ ] Alberti bass   [✓] Atonal

Question 8

Higher Music concept: (a) Listen to this excerpt and identify the style of the music. _Mass Oratorio_

National 5 concepts: (b) Listen to the excerpt again and tick **two** boxes to describe features present

[✓] Homophonic   [ ] Backing vocals   [ ] Ground bass

[ ] Snare drum   [ ] A Cappella   [✓] Timpani

Question 9

Higher Music concept: (a) Listen to this excerpt and identify the style of the music. _Musique Concrète_

Question 10

Higher music concept: (a) Listen to this excerpt and identify the style of the music. _String quartet Romantic_

National 5 concepts: (b) Listen to the excerpt again and tick **two** boxes to describe features present

[ ] Walking bass   [✓] Cadenza   [✓] Pizzicato

[✓] Accelerando   [ ] Pentatonic scale   [ ] Compound time

Question 11

Higher Music concept: (a) Listen to this excerpt and identify the style of the music. Soul Jazzfunk

National 5 concepts: (b) Listen to the excerpt again and tick **two** boxes to describe features present

☑ Backing vocals   ☑ Snare drum   ☐ Ritardando

☐ Sequence   ☐ Canon   ☑ Riff

 Activity!

Set a listening test for your fellow students

Select a few pieces or excerpts of music based on Higher Music **STYLE** concepts (possibly sourced online) and play them to your fellow students to see if they can identify the concept that describes their **STYLE**. They can do the same to test you, but of course in choosing the music for this exercise you will have already taken part in a listening exercise!

Note: You can carry out this type of listening exercise for each unit in this chapter.

 Great advice... **Top Tip**

A process of elimination

When you have to identify, from a list, a number of concepts present in a musical excerpt, rather than try to listen for *specific* concepts from the list during the first listening, you might find it helpful to make a quick note of the *obvious* features you hear in the music, then compare this with the options on the question paper. Any features from your notes which match those on the list will almost certainly be correct answers.

Another method is to begin by eliminating from the list those features which you think are definitely NOT present, leaving you with a shorter list of possible correct answers.

Unit 2 MELODY/HARMONY Concepts

Higher Music MELODY/HARMONY concepts

• Mode / Modal	• Mordent	• Diminished triad
• Relative major / minor	• Plagal cadence	• Diminished 7th
• Interval	• Interrupted cadence	• Added 6th
• Obliggato (instrumental)	• Tierce de Picardie	• Harmonic minor scale
• Acciaccatura	• Dominant 7th	• Melodic minor scale

 Activity!

Brainstorm

Write down or discuss with your classmates what you know about the above **MELODY/HARMONY** concepts and consider whether you would be able to recognise each one by ear. Things to think about are: the main characteristic(s) of each concept and, where appropriate, the names of any particular songs/pieces you know which contain or represent a concept, together with their composer(s). Your descriptions needn't be too detailed; single words or brief explanations may be enough. For definitions of each concept, or just to refresh your memory, refer to the Glossary section.

 Listen in

The musical excerpts for use with this unit are on the video, *'Higher Music concept excerpts for unit 2'*, which can be accessed by clicking on the audio icon above (e-book) or on the jm-education YouTube channel at *www.youtube/jm-education*.

- **Read through each question before listening to the music.**

- **The number of times each excerpt will be played is indicated in the question.**

 Take Note

In this unit's exercises (questions 1 to 9) you will have to identify Higher Music **MELODY/HARMONY** concepts (no other Higher Music concepts will feature), together with general National 5 Music concepts.

The questions will be in a varied format, reflecting those found in the final examination question paper. (see Chapter 3).

* **Answers to the exercises in this unit are on page 132.**

Unit 2. MELODY/HARMONY concepts listening exercises

Question 1

Listen to this excerpt and identify **four** concepts in the music from those listed below. Read through the concepts before hearing the music. The music will be played **three times** with a pause of 10 seconds between playings and a pause of 40 seconds before the next question starts.

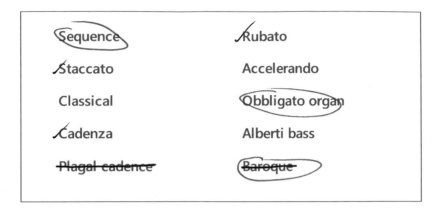

~~Sequence~~	Rubato
Staccato	Accelerando
Classical	Obbligato organ
Cadenza	Alberti bass
~~Plagal cadence~~	~~Baroque~~

Insert your **four** answers on the lines below.

Rubato

Staccato

Cadenza

Alberti bass ?

Question 2

(a) Listen to this excerpt and identify **three** concepts in the music from those listed below. Read through the concepts before hearing the music. The music will be played **twice** with a pause of 10 seconds between playings and a pause of 40 seconds before the next question starts.

~~Strathspey~~	Anacrusis
Mode/modal	Cross rhythms
~~Classical~~	Strophic
Contrary motion	Alto voice
A cappella	

Insert your **three** answers on the lines below.

A cappella

Model modal

Alto voice

(b) Listen to a continuation of this excerpt and name the folk percussion instrument playing. The music will be played **once**.

Bodhran ?

Question 3

Listen to this excerpt and identify **four** concepts in the music from those listed below. Read through the concepts before hearing the music. The music will be played **three times** with a pause of 10 seconds between playings and a pause of 40 seconds before the next question starts.

Pedal   Pentatonic scale

Countermelody   ~~Major key~~

Mordent   Cadenza

Cluster chord   Pause

Perfect cadence   ~~Harpsichord~~

Insert your **four** answers on the lines below.

Mordent

Pause

Pedal

Perfect cadence

Question 4

This question features instrumental music. A guide to the music is shown below. You are required to complete this guide by inserting music concepts. Read through the question before listening to the music. The music will be played **three times** with a pause of 20 seconds between playings. You will then have a further 30 seconds to complete your answer.

---

1. The ornament played by the brass instruments is a/an

 _acciaccatura ?/_____

2. The three percussion instruments heard in the excerpt are

 timpani
 1. _Glockenspiel_   2. _triangle/_   3. _?_ _cymbal_

3. An Italian term that describes what happens to the tempo near the end of the excerpt is

 _Rallentando ✓_____

4. The music is in _forte? triple_ metre.

5. The music is an excerpt from a symphony from the _20ᵗʰ cent._ period.
 romantic

Question 5

(a) Listen to this excerpt and identify **three** concepts in the music from those listed below. Read through the concepts before hearing the music. The music will be played **twice** with a pause of 10 seconds between playings and a pause of 40 seconds before the next question starts.

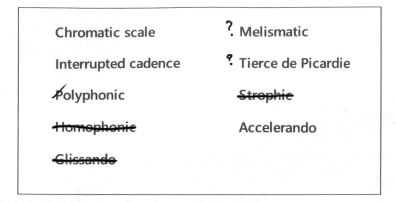

Insert your **three** answers on the lines below.

Polyphonic

Tierce de Picarde

Melismatic

(b) Listen to another excerpt and describe which type of minor scale (**harmonic** or **melodic**) was used for the notes in this piece of music. The music will be played **once**.

Melodic

Question 6

Listen to this excerpt and identify **three** concepts in the music from those listed below. Read through the concepts before hearing the music. The music will be played **twice** with a pause of 10 seconds between playings and a pause of 40 seconds before the next question starts.

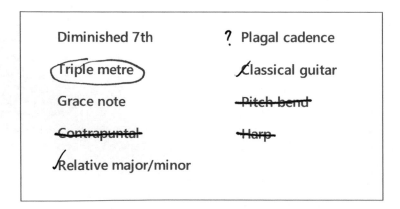

Insert your **three** answers on the lines below.

Classical guitar

Relative major/minor

Plagal cadence

Question 7

Listen to this excerpt and identify **four** concepts in the music from those listed below. Read through the concepts before hearing the music. The music will be played **three times** with a pause of 10 seconds between playings and a pause of 40 seconds before the next question starts.

Riff	Distortion
? Triple metre	Acoustic guitar
Electric guitar	Atonal
Whole tone scale	? Harmonic minor
Rallentando	Celtic rock

Insert your **four** answers on the lines below.

Electric guitar

Distortion

Harmonic minor

Riff

Question 8

(a) Listen to the following short excerpt and tick **one** box to identify the **second last** chord you hear. The music will be played **twice** with a pause of 10 seconds between playings and 20 seconds before question 8(b) starts.

- [x] Dominant 7th
- [ ] Minor
- [ ] Diminished 7th
- [ ] Added 6th

(b) Listen to the following short excerpt and tick **one** box to identify the **last** chord you hear. The music will be played **twice** with a pause of 10 seconds between playings and 20 seconds before question 8(c) starts.

- [ ] Diminished 7th
- [x] Added 6th
- [ ] Dominant 7th
- [ ] Major

(c) Listen to the following short excerpt and tick **one** box to identify the **last** chord you hear. The music will be played **twice** with a pause of 10 seconds between playings and 20 seconds before the next question starts.

- ☐ Major
- ☑ Diminished 7th
- ☐ Added 6th
- ☐ Dominant 7th

Question 9

(a) Listen to the following short excerpt and tick **one** box to describe the cadence you hear. The music will be played **twice** with a pause of 10 seconds between playings and 20 seconds before question 9(b) starts.

- ☐ Perfect cadence
- ☑ Plagal cadence
- ☐ Interrupted cadence
- ☐ Imperfect cadence

(b) Listen to the following short excerpt and tick **one** box to describe the cadence you hear. The music will be played **twice** with a pause of 10 seconds between playings and 20 seconds before question 9(c) starts.

- ☐ Perfect cadence
- ☐ Plagal cadence
- ☑ Interrupted cadence
- ☐ Imperfect cadence

(c) Listen to the following short excerpt and tick **one** box to describe the cadence you hear. The music will be played **twice** with a pause of 10 seconds between playings and 20 seconds after the second playing.

- ☑ Perfect cadence
- ☐ Plagal cadence
- ☐ Interrupted cadence
- ☐ Imperfect cadence

Unit 3 RHYTHM/TEMPO Concepts

Higher Music RHYTHM/TEMPO concepts

• 3 against 2	• Irregular time signatures	• Augmentation
• Time changes	• Diminution	• Triplets

 **Activity!**

Brainstorm

Write down or discuss with your classmates what you know about the above **RHYTHM/TEMPO** concepts and consider whether you would be able to recognise each one by ear. Things to think about are: the main characteristic(s) of each concept and, where appropriate, the names of any particular songs/pieces you know which contain or represent a concept, together with their composer(s). Your descriptions needn't be too detailed; single words or brief explanations may be enough. For definitions of each concept, or just to refresh your memory, refer to the Glossary section.

 Listen in

The musical excerpts for use with this unit are on the video, *'Higher Music concept excerpts for unit 3'*, which can be accessed by clicking on the audio icon above (e-book) or on the jm-education YouTube channel at *www.youtube/jm-education*.

- **Read through each question before listening to the music.**

- **The number of times each excerpt will be played is indicated in the question.**

 Take Note

In this unit's exercises (questions 1 to 5) you will have to identify Higher Music **RHYTHM/TEMPO** concepts (no other Higher Music concepts will feature), together with general National 5 Music concepts.

The questions will be in a varied format, reflecting those used in the final examination question paper (see Chapter 3).

* **Answers to the exercises in this unit are on page 132.**

Unit 3. RHYTHM/TEMPO concepts listening exercises

www.youtube.com/jm-education

Question 1

Listen to this excerpt and identify **four** concepts in the music from those listed below. Read through the concepts before hearing the music. The music will be played **three times** with a pause of 10 seconds between playings and a pause of 40 seconds before the next question starts.

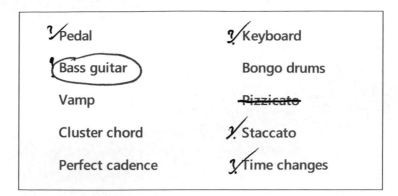

? Pedal   ? Keyboard

(Bass guitar)   Bongo drums

Vamp   Pizzicato

Cluster chord   ? Staccato

Perfect cadence   ? Time changes

Insert your **four** answers on the lines below.

Time changes
Keyboard
Pedal
Staccato

Question 2

Listen to this excerpt and identify **four** concepts in the music from those listed below. Read through the concepts before hearing the music. The music will be played **three times** with a pause of 10 seconds between playings and a pause of 40 seconds before the next question starts.

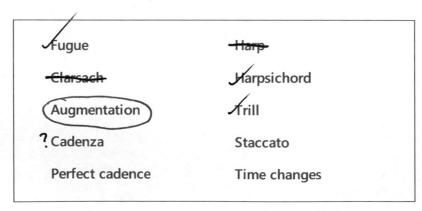

Fugue   Harp

Clarsach   Harpsichord

(Augmentation)   Trill

? Cadenza   Staccato

Perfect cadence   Time changes

Insert your **four** answers on the lines below.

Harpsichord
Trill
Fugue
Cadenza

Question 3

Listen to this excerpt and identify **three** concepts in the music from those listed below. Read through the concepts before hearing the music. The music will be played **twice** with a pause of 10 seconds between playings and a pause of 40 seconds before the next question starts.

~~Scat singing~~   ? Key change

? Triple metre   ~~Classical guitar~~

~~Saxophone~~   Strophic

Anacrusis   ? Riff

? 3 against 2

Insert your **three** answers on the lines below.

3 against 2

Key change

Riff

Question 4

Listen to this excerpt and identify **four** concepts in the music from those listed below. Read through the concepts before hearing the music. The music will be played **three times** with a pause of 10 seconds between playings and a pause of 40 seconds before the next question starts.

Tempo change   ? Minimalist

~~Bass guitar~~   ~~Sitar~~

Classical   ? Irregular Time signatures

Ground bass   ? Imitation

? Pizzicato   Trill

Insert your **four** answers on the lines below.

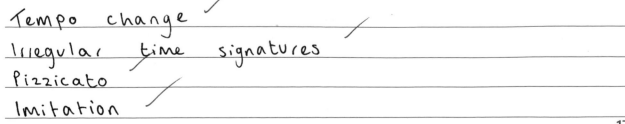

Tempo change

Irregular time signatures

Pizzicato

Imitation

Question 5

This question features instrumental music. A guide to the music is shown below. You are required to complete this guide by inserting music concepts. Read through the question before listening to the music. The music will be played **three times** with a pause of 20 seconds between playings. You will then have a further 30 seconds to complete your answer.

1.   The instrument playing the melody is a/an _Violin_ ✓

2.   A concept that describes the playing technique used by this instrument is _arco_ ✓

3.   The keyboard instrument heard in the accompaniment is a _harpsichord_ ✓

4.   The Time Signature can be described as _simple?_   _4/4_ ✓

5.   Parts of the melody are repeated in shorter note values as the music progresses. This is known as

     diminution ✓

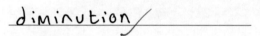
Great advice... **Top Tip**

When you have to identify, from a list, a number of concepts present in a musical excerpt (in Listening test question papers, for example), rather than try to listen for specific concepts from the list during the first listening, you may find it helpful to make a quick note of the OBVIOUS features you hear in the music, then compare this with the options on the question paper. Any features from your notes which match those on the question paper will surely be correct answers.

Another method is to begin by eliminating from the list those features which you think are definitely NOT present, leaving you with a shorter list of possible correct answers.

You only have a certain amount of time to answer questions in a Listening test so, whichever methods you find most effective for identifying musical concepts in a piece of music, just make sure you have a well-practised strategy before tackling any exam!

Unit 4 TEXTURE/STRUCTURE/FORM Concepts

Higher Music TEXTURE/STRUCTURE/FORM concepts

• Through-composed	• Concerto grosso	• Basso continuo
• Da Capo aria	• Sonata form	• Ritornello
• Passacaglia	• Exposition	• Subject

 Activity!

Brainstorm

Write down or discuss with your classmates what you know about the above **TEXTURE/STRUCTURE/FORM** concepts and consider whether you would be able to recognise each one by ear. Things to think about are: the main characteristic(s) of each concept and, where appropriate, the names of any particular songs/pieces you know which contain or represent a concept, together with their composer(s). Your descriptions needn't be too detailed; single words or brief explanations may be enough. For definitions of each concept, or just to refresh your memory, refer to the Glossary section.

 Listen in

The musical excerpts for use with this unit are on the video, **'Higher Music concept excerpts for unit 4'**, which can be accessed by clicking on the audio icon above (e-book) or on the jm-education YouTube channel at **www.youtube/jm-education**.

- **Read through each question before listening to the music.**

- **The number of times each excerpt will be played is indicated in the question.**

 Take Note

In this unit's exercises (questions 1 to 7) you will have to identify Higher Music **TEXTURE/STRUCTURE/FORM** concepts (no other Higher Music concepts will feature), together with general National 5 Music concepts.

The questions will be in a varied format, reflecting those used in the final examination question paper (see Chapter 3).

* **Answers to the exercises in this unit are on page 133.**

Unit 4. TEXTURE/STRUCTURE/FORM concepts listening exercises

www.youtube.com/jm-education

Question 1

Listen to this excerpt and identify **four** concepts in the music from those listed below. Read through the concepts before hearing the music. The music will be played **three times** with a pause of 10 seconds between playings and a pause of 40 seconds before the next question starts.

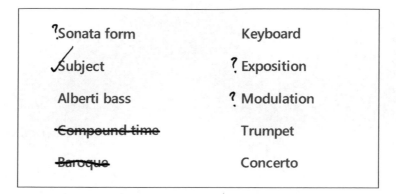

? Sonata form	Keyboard
✓ Subject	? Exposition
Alberti bass	? Modulation
~~Compound time~~	Trumpet
~~Baroque~~	Concerto

Insert your **four** answers on the lines below.

Subject

Modulation

Exposition

Sonata form

Question 2

Listen to a continuation of this excerpt and identify **three** concepts in the music from those listed below. Read through the concepts before hearing the music. The music will be played **twice** with a pause of 10 seconds between playings and a pause of 40 seconds before the next question starts.

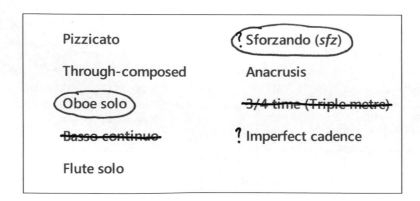

Pizzicato	? Sforzando (*sfz*)
Through-composed	Anacrusis
Oboe solo	~~3/4 time (Triple metre)~~
~~Basso continuo~~	? Imperfect cadence
Flute solo	

Insert your **three** answers on the lines below.

Flute solo

Imperfect cadence

Through - composed

Question 3

Listen to this excerpt and identify **four** concepts in the music from those listed below. Read through the concepts before hearing the music. The music will be played **three** times with a pause of 10 seconds between playings and a pause of 40 seconds before the next question starts.

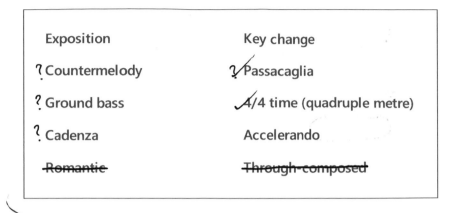

Insert your **four** answers on the lines below.

Passacaglia

4/4 time

Counter melody

Ground bass

Question 4

Listen to this excerpt and identify **four** concepts in the music from those listed below. Read through the concepts before hearing the music. The music will be played **three times** with a pause of 10 seconds between playings and a pause of 40 seconds before the next question starts.

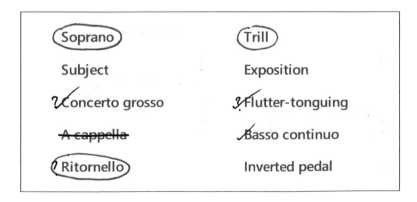

Insert your **four** answers on the lines below.

Concerto grosso

Flutter tonguing

Basso continuo

Subject

Question 5

Listen to a continuation of the previous excerpt and identify **four** concepts in the music from those listed below. Read through the concepts before hearing the music. The music will be played **three times** with a pause of 10 seconds between playings and a pause of 40 seconds before the next question starts.

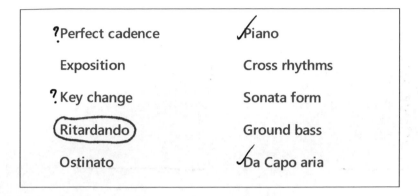

Insert your **four** answers on the lines below.

Da Capo aria

Piano

Perfect cadence

Key change

Question 6

Listen to this excerpt and identify **four** concepts in the music from those listed below. Read through the concepts before hearing the music. The music will be played **three times** with a pause of 10 seconds between playings and a pause of 40 seconds before the next question starts.

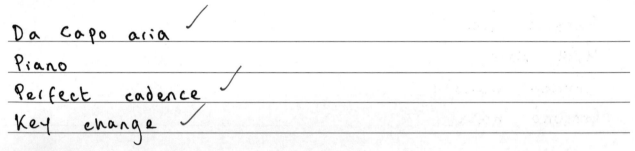

Insert your **four** answers on the lines below.

Metre change

Imitation

Con sordino

Discord

Question 7

Listen to this excerpt and identify **three** concepts in the music from those listed below. Read through the concepts before hearing the music. The music will be played **twice** with a pause of 10 seconds between playings and a pause of 40 seconds before the next question starts.

Bass voice	Countermelody
?Tenor voice	Da Capo aria
Alberti bass	? Key change
Cello	Through-composed
?Vamp	

Insert your **three** answers on the lines below.

Key change

Tenor voice

Through - composed

⭐ **Activity!**

A little bit of self-help

For you and your fellow students to test yourselves, why not choose a selection of music and set your own tests for each other using the exercises in this chapter as a guide? It's more interesting that way, and great practice for Listening tests!

Unit 5 TIMBRE/DYNAMICS Concepts

Higher Music TIMBRE/DYNAMICS concepts

● Tremolando / tremolo	● Ripieno
● Harmonics	● Concertino
● Coloratura	● String quartet

 **Activity!**

Brainstorm

Write down or discuss with your classmates what you know about the above **TIMBRE/DYNAMICS** concepts and consider whether you would be able to recognise each one by ear. Things to think about are: the main characteristic(s) of each concept and, where appropriate, the names of any particular songs/pieces you know which contain or represent a concept, together with their composer(s). Your descriptions needn't be too detailed; single words or brief explanations may be enough. For definitions of each concept, or just to refresh your memory, refer to the Glossary section.

 Listen in

The musical excerpts for use with this unit are on the video, *'Higher Music concept excerpts for unit 5'*, which can be accessed by clicking on the audio icon above (e-book) or on the jm-education YouTube channel at *www.youtube/jm-education*.

- **Read through each question before listening to the music.**

- **The number of times each excerpt will be played is indicated in the question.**

 Take Note

In this unit's exercises (questions 1 to 5) you will have to identify Higher Music **TIMBRE/DYNAMICS** concepts (no other Higher Music concepts will feature), together with general National 5 Music concepts.

The questions will be in a varied format, reflecting those used in the final examination question paper (see Chapter 3).

* Answers to the exercises in this unit are on page 133.

Unit 5. TIMBRE/DYNAMICS concepts listening exercises

(Question 1)

www.youtube.com/jm-education

Listen to this excerpt and identify **four** concepts in the music from those listed below. Read through the concepts before hearing the music. The music will be played **three times** with a pause of 10 seconds between playings and a pause of 40 seconds before the next question starts.

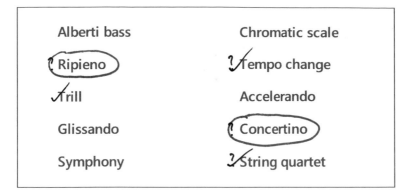

Alberti bass	Chromatic scale
Ripieno	? Tempo change
Trill	Accelerando
Glissando	Concertino
Symphony	String quartet

Insert your **four** answers on the lines below.

Trill

Tempo change

String quartet

Chromatic scale ?

(Question 2)

Listen to this excerpt and identify **four** concepts in the music from those listed below. Read through the concepts before hearing the music. The music will be played **three times** with a pause of 10 seconds between playings and a pause of 40 seconds before the next question starts.

? Legato	Concerto
Crescendo	? Timpani roll
Harmonics	Accelerando
Triple metre	Snare drum
Pizzicato	Tremolando/tremolo

Insert your **four** answers on the lines below.

Timpani roll

Legato

Tremolando

Crescendo

Question 3

This question features vocal music. A guide to the music is shown below. You are required to complete this guide by inserting music concepts. Read through the question before listening to the music. The music will be played **three times** with a pause of 20 seconds between playings. You will then have a further 30 seconds to complete your answer before the next question starts.

1. Tick one box to describe the voice range of the singer

    ☑ Tenor   ☐ Alto   ☑ Soprano   ☑ Baritone

2. The concept that describes the decorative singing technique featured is

    Coloratura ✓

3. This song comes from a larger composition known as a/an ___aria ?___

4. A song from this type of larger work is called a/an ___opera ?___

5. The cadence at the end of the excerpt is a/an ___perfect ✓___ cadence

Question 4

Listen to this excerpt and identify **three** concepts in the music from those listed below. Read through the concepts before hearing the music. The music will be played **twice** with a pause of 10 seconds between playings and a pause of 40 seconds before the next question starts.

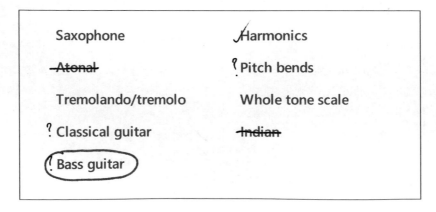

Saxophone	Harmonics ✓
~~Atonal~~	? Pitch bends
Tremolando/tremolo	Whole tone scale
? Classical guitar	~~Indian~~
(! Bass guitar)	

Insert your **three** answers on the lines below.

Harmonics ✓

Pitch bends ✓

Classical guitar

Question 5

Listen to this excerpt and identify **four** concepts in the music from those listed below. Read through the concepts before hearing the music. The music will be played **three times** with a pause of 10 seconds between playings and a pause of 40 seconds before the next question starts.

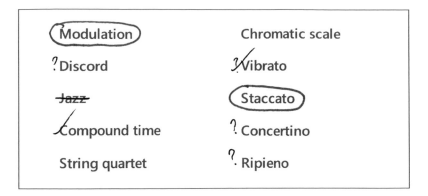

Insert your **four** answers on the lines below.

Compound time
Vibrato
String quartet
chromatic scale

Great advice...
Top Tip

A good way to keep your listening skills sharp is to practise making notes about what you hear every time you listen to a piece of music. Start by listening for obvious features like **structure**, **tonality** (**major** or **minor**), **metre** and **style**, then, during the second listening, try to pick out details such as individual instruments, **dynamics**, **melodic** features (**ornaments**, **staccato**, **legato** etc.) and **texture**. The more you practise this, the quicker you will become at identifying the important features in any kind of music.

Chapter 2 Music Literacy

Literacy requirements for Higher Music

In addition to knowledge of a wide range of musical concepts, the Higher Music course requires that you understand the elements of music literacy (or music theory) outlined in this chapter. There will be a question based on these literacy elements in the final question paper (usually question 3 or 4), so everything you specifically need to know is summarised in the chart below, with music notation examples given on pages 29-38. Two sample exercises then follow, containing questions similar to those that will feature in the exam. (See also question 4 of the *Specimen question paper* in chapter 3 as a further example.)

 **Take Note**

It will be helpful to also revise National 5 music literacy requirements before tackling this chapter - see the *Glossary* section (pages 130-131) for a summary of these.

Higher Music Literacy Requirements

- **Notes on the bass clef from E (below the stave) up to middle C**

- **Transposing notes in treble clef down one octave into bass clef**

- **Identifying tonic, subdominant and dominant notes in the keys of C, G and F major and A minor**

- **Identifying chords I, IV, V and VI in major and minor keys in both treble and bass clefs**

- **Naming diatonic intervals: 2nd, 3rd, 4th, 5th, 6th, 7th, octave**

- **Writing diatonic intervals above a given note in treble clef**

- **Rests: whole bar, semibreve, minim, dotted crotchet, crotchet, quaver**

- **Slurs, accents, staccato dots, phrase marks**

- **Dotted minims, dotted crotchets, crotchets and quavers within 6/8, 9/8 and 12/8 time**

- **Triplet crotchets and triplet quavers**

- **Da Capo (D.C.)**

The tasks you will typically be expected to undertake are:

- **Transpose** a small part of a **melody** in **treble clef** down an **octave** into **bass clef**

- Describe the **interval** between two notes printed on the music as a **2nd**, **3rd**, **4th**, **5th** etc.

- Identify the **key** or **time signature** of the piece

- Identify the **ornament** heard (Trill, Mordent, Acciaccatura, Grace note)

- Correct the **rhythm** printed on the music to match what you actually hear

- Write the **notes** heard in the music but missing on the music notation (three to five notes)

- Insert missing **bars** or **rests**

- Name the **chords** you hear using either letter names (e.g. **C**, **F**, **G**, **Am**) or Roman numbers (e.g. **I**, **IV**, **V**, **VI**)

Note: you may also be required to identify other music literacy features that are specific to the grade (see previous page).

There now follows a succession of explanations and diagrams to help you with these areas of music literacy (which you can use for quick reference), followed by two sample literacy questions similar to those found in the Higher Music question paper.

Notes on the Bass Clef

Notes on the **bass clef** from **E** below the stave up to **middle C** (notes on the **treble clef** are also given for reference).

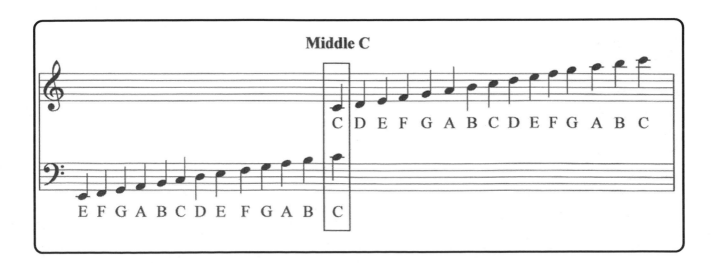

Transposing notes in Treble Clef down one octave into Bass Clef

In the examples below, the music in **treble clef** is shown transposed down **one octave** into **bass clef**. The process would of course simply be reversed if transposing up **one octave** from **bass clef** into **treble clef**.

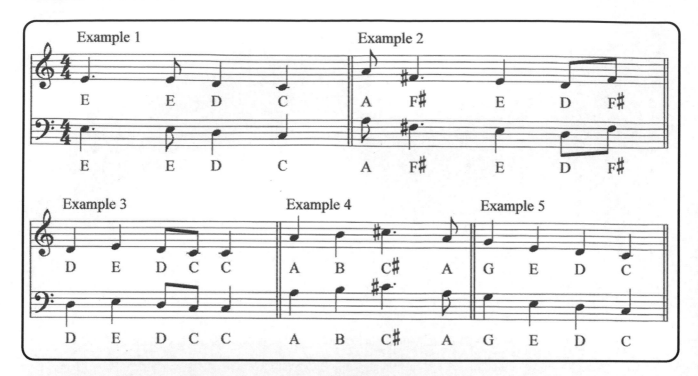

Identifying Tonic, Subdominant and Dominant notes in the Keys of C, G and F major and A minor

Tonic, **Subdominant** and **Dominant** are the names given to notes 1, 4 and 5 of a **scale**.

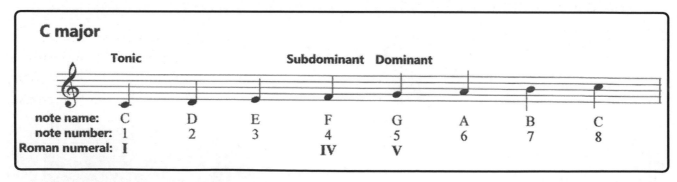

Tonic, **Subdominant** and **Dominant** in the **key** of **G major**.

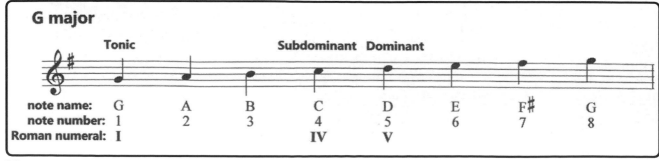

Tonic, **Subdominant** and **Dominant** in the **key** of **F major**.

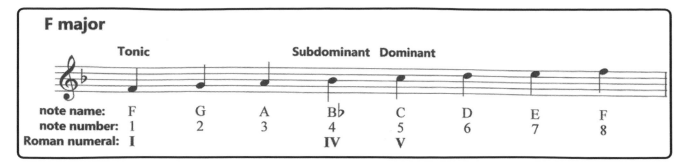

Tonic, **Subdominant** and **Dominant** in the **key** of **A minor**.

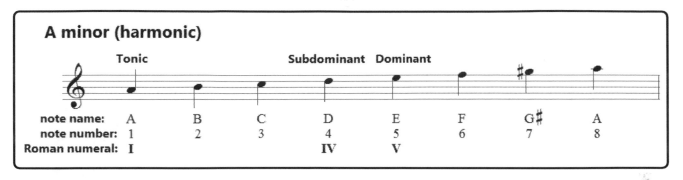

Identifying Chords I, IV, V and VI in Major and Minor Keys in both Treble and Bass Clefs

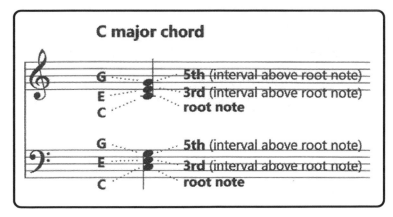

A basic **chord** is made up of three notes (a *triad*): the '**root**' note on the bottom, followed by the notes a **third** and **fifth** (**interval**) above. So, the **chord** of **C major** has **C** as the **root** note, with the notes **E** (a **third** higher than **C**) and **G** (a **fifth** higher than **C**) above.

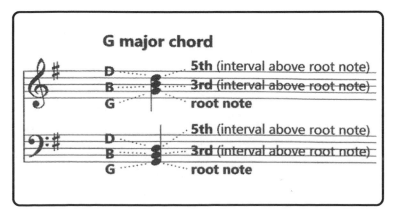

The chord of **G major** has **G** as the **root** note, with the notes **B** (a **third** higher than **G**) and **D** (a **fifth** higher than **G**) above.

All basic *triads* are made in this way, in both **major** and **minor** keys. So, to construct a **chord**, just think of the **key** and **scale** of that **chord** and use the *first*, *third* and *fifth* notes of that **scale** to make the **chord**. When doing this, however, the **key signature** MUST be taken into account, too! For example, to make a **D major chord** we must remember that the **key signature** of **D major** has **F sharp** and **C sharp**, so these notes must remain sharp if they occur in any notes of the **chord**.

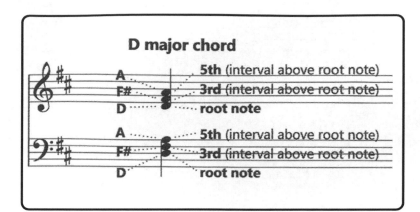

The **root** or first note of a **D major chord** is **D**, the note a **third** above **D** is **F sharp** (because **F sharp** is in the **key signature**), and the note a **fifth** above **D** is **A**.

Chords can be built on any note of a **scale** and are often indicated by Roman numerals (numbers) to show the note in the **scale** from which they originate. The following examples have **chords I**, **IV**, **V** and **VI** highlighted for clarity.

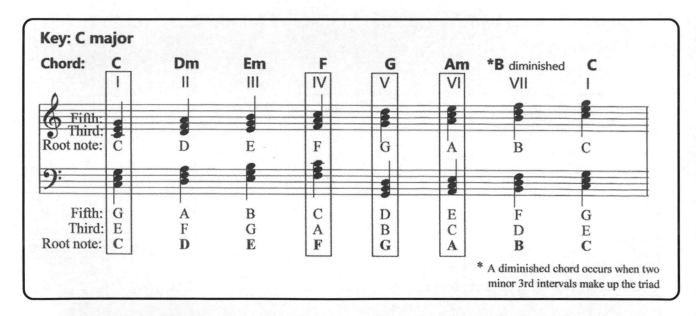

* A diminished chord occurs when two minor 3rd intervals make up the triad

🔊 **Listen in**

Chords I, IV, V & VI in C major

To hear chords **I**, **IV**, **V** and **VI** in the **key** of **C major**, click on the audio icon above (e-book), or access the video, '***Chords I, IV, V and VI in the key of C major***' on the jm-education YouTube channel at ***www.youtube/jm-education***.

Note: the YouTube video contains various examples of these **chords** playing in different combinations, as well as some helpful tips for recognising them by ear.

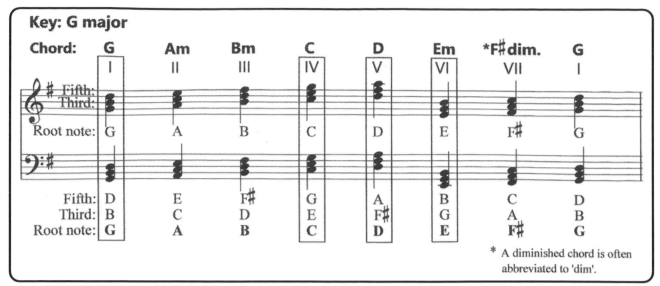

Listen in

Chords I, IV, V & VI in G major

To hear chords **I**, **IV**, **V** and **VI** in the **key** of **G major**, click on the audio icon above (e-book), or access the video, '*Chords I, IV, V and VI in the key of G major*' on the jm-education YouTube channel at ***www.youtube/jm-education***.

Note: the YouTube video contains various examples of these **chords** playing in different combinations, as well as some helpful tips for recognising them by ear.

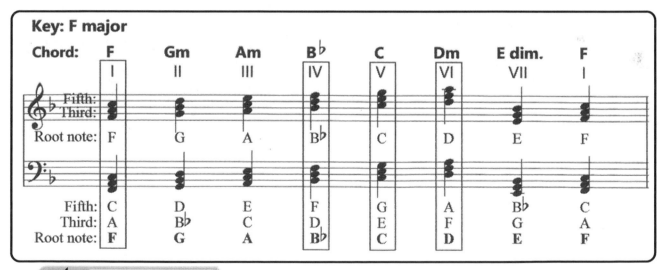

Listen in

Chords I, IV, V & VI in F major

To hear chords **I**, **IV**, **V** and **VI** in the **key** of **F major**, click on the audio icon above (e-book), or access the video, '*Chords I, IV, V and VI in the key of F major*' on the jm-education YouTube channel at ***www.youtube/jm-education***.

Note: the YouTube video contains various examples of these **chords** playing in different combinations, as well as some helpful tips for recognising them by ear.

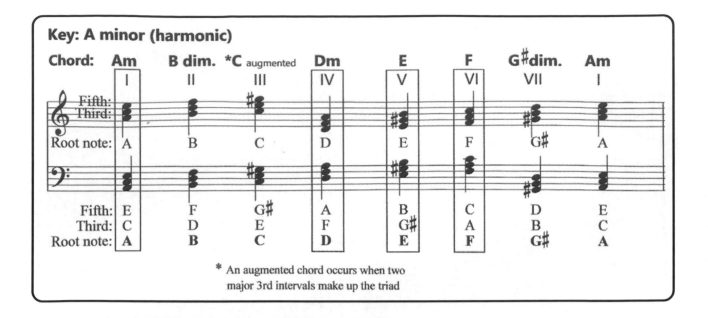

Key: A minor (harmonic)

* An augmented chord occurs when two
major 3rd intervals make up the triad

 Listen in

Chords I, IV, V & VI in A minor

To hear chords **I**, **IV**, **V** and **VI** in the **key** of **A minor**, click on the audio icon above (e-book), or access the video, '**Chords I, IV, V and VI in the key of A minor**' on the jm-education YouTube channel at **www.youtube/jm-education**.

Note: the YouTube video contains various examples of these **chords** playing in different combinations, as well as some helpful tips for recognising them by ear.

Great advice...

Top Tip

Major and Minor Chord Patterns

Because of the ordering of **intervals** in the construction of **chords**, the following pattern occurs in every **major key**:

- MAJOR KEY: chords I, IV and V are MAJOR chords, and chord VI is a MINOR chord

Minor keys are more variable because there are different versions of the **minor scale** (e.g. **harmonic minor**, **melodic minor**, **pentatonic minor** and **natural minor** scales), but if we use the **harmonic minor scale** as a guide, the following **chord** pattern occurs:

- MINOR (HARMONIC) KEY: chords I and IV are MINOR chords, and chords V and VI are MAJOR chords

Naming Diatonic Intervals: 2nd, 3rd, 4th, 5th, 6th, 7th, octave

The term 'diatonic interval' simply refers to the distance between two notes which are in the same **scale** or **key**. So, in the **key** or **scale** of **C major**, for example, the **interval** between the notes **C** and **E** is a **3rd**, because there are three (**ascending**) notes involved in the **interval** (C, D, E). Similarly, in the same **scale**, the **interval** between the notes **C** and **B** is a **7th** because there are seven (**ascending**) notes involved in the **interval** (C, D, E, F, G, A, B).

Note: when calculating an interval we always count *upwards* from the lowest note to the highest.

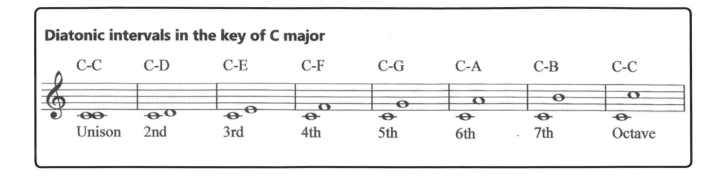

Writing Diatonic Intervals above a given note in Treble Clef

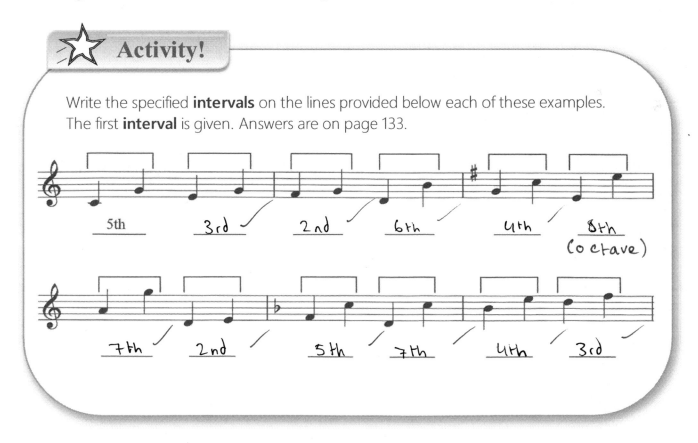

Rests: whole bar, semibreve, minim, dotted crotchet, crotchet and quaver

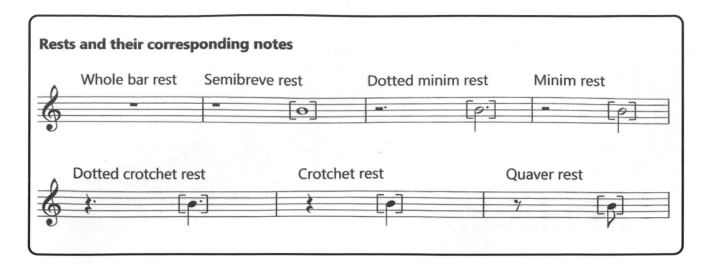

Rests and their corresponding notes

Whole bar rest   Semibreve rest   Dotted minim rest   Minim rest

Dotted crotchet rest   Crotchet rest   Quaver rest

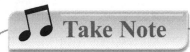

Take Note

A **whole bar rest** looks identical to a **semibreve rest**, but this doesn't cause confusion since no other notes (or rests) will appear in a bar containing a **whole bar rest,** whereas a bar containing a **semibreve rest** will always need other notes or rests to make it complete.

Slurs, Accents, Staccato dots, Phrase marks

1. Slurs   2. Accents   3. Staccato dots   4. Phrase marks

1. **Slur**. Indicated by a curved line between (usually) two - or more - *different* notes, a slur means that notes have to be played as smoothly as possible, one after the other, with no discernible separation between the two, as though one note merges into the other.

2. **Accent**. Indicated by a symbol resembling an arrow head, an accent means that notes should be played with strong emphasis.

3. **Staccato dots**. Indicated by a dot above the note head, staccato dots mean that notes have to be played in a short, detached way, with their duration cut shorter than that indicated - in a way sometimes described as being similar to the sound of distant gun fire.

4. **Phrase marks**. Indicated by a long, curved line over a passage of notes, phrase marks show individual musical phrases which should be expressed rather like spoken statements (in a conversation), with tiny 'breaths' inferred between each phrase.

Dotted minims, dotted crotchets, crotchets and quavers within 6/8, 9/8 and 12/8 time

In the **compound time signatures** of **6/8**, **9/8** and **12/8** time, **quavers** receive one complete beat - as opposed to half a beat, as in **simple time signatures** such as **2/4**, **3/4** and **4/4** time. This means that **crotchets** receive *two* beats, **dotted crotchets** *three* beats and **dotted minims** *six* beats.

In **compound time** the notes are also arranged in groups of three rather than two or four (as in **simple time**). **Note**: in the examples below the main beats are shown as bold numbers below each bar.

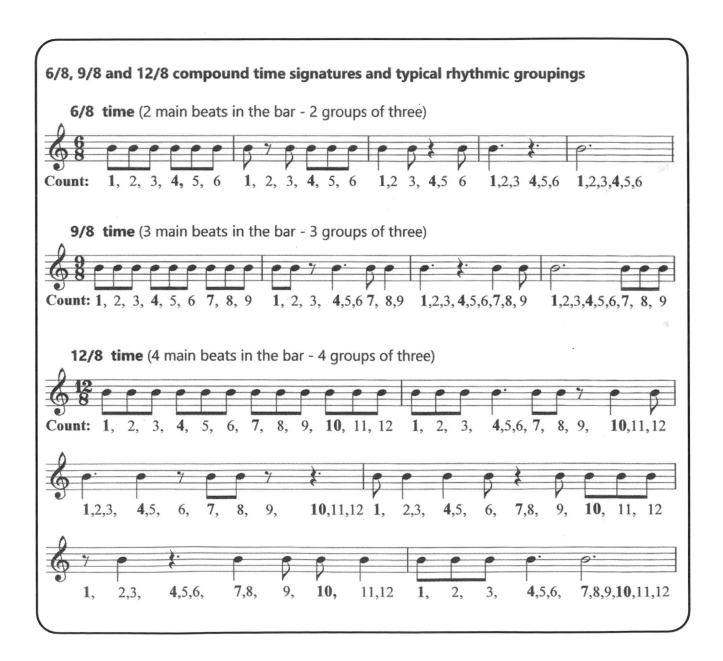

Triplet crotchets and triplet quavers

Triplet crotchets occur when three **crotchets** are played evenly in the time of two **crotchet** beats (see example below). This is also known as **3 against 2**.

Triplet quavers occur when three **quavers** are played evenly in the space of one **crotchet** beat (see example below).

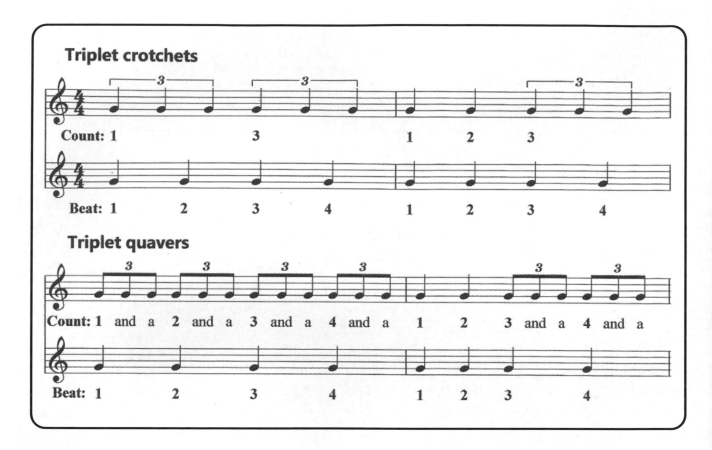

Da Capo (D.C.)

The instruction **Da Capo** means return to the beginning of the piece and continue playing from there. The term is usually abbreviated to **D.C.** You will often see the instruction **D.C. Al Coda** (meaning go back to the beginning and play through to the **Coda** (end section)), or **D.C. Al Fine** (meaning go back to the beginning and play until **Al Fine**, the point where the piece should end).

Specimen Music Literacy questions

There now follows two Music Literacy exercises in the same format as (usually) Question 3 or 4 of the Higher Music question paper.

Music Literacy exercise 1

The audio component for this exercise can be accessed by clicking on the audio icon above (e-book), or by accessing the video 'Higher Music Literacy exercise 1' on the jm-education YouTube channel at *www.youtube/jm-education*. Answers are on page 133.

Exercise 1

This question is based on an arrangement of traditional music.

Listen to the excerpt and follow the guide to the music on the next page.

Here is the music for the first time.

You now have two minutes to read the question.

All answers must be written in (or below) the boxes on the next page.

(a) Insert the time signature in the correct place in the box.

(b) Correct the rhythm in **bar 5** to match what you hear. Use the given blank bar.

(c) Describe the interval formed by the first two notes in **bar 7**. Write your answer on the line in the box.

(d) Transpose **bar 9 one octave lower** into the bass clef. Use the given blank bar.

(e) Insert the missing notes on the empty stave in **bar 12**. The rhythm is given.

(f) Name the **chords** used in the final cadence in bars 16-17. You may use letter names (e.g. F, Am, C, G) or numbers (e.g. I, IV, V, VI). Write your answers on the lines in the box. An example is given in bar 15.

Choose from the following: C   Chord I
                               F   Chord IV
                               G   Chord V
                               Am   Chord VI

During the next three playings complete your answers (a) to (f).

The music will be played **three** more times with a pause of 30 seconds between playings and two minutes at the end to complete your answer.

Here is the music for the second time.

Here is the music for the third time.

Here is the music for the fourth time.

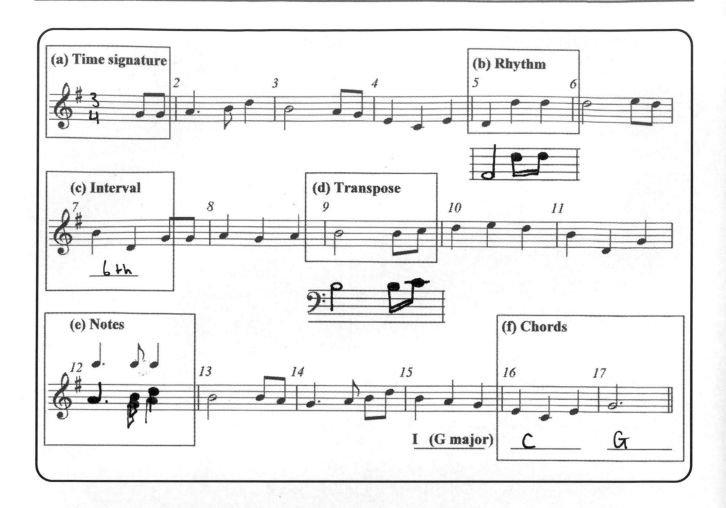

Listen in

Music Literacy exercise 2

The audio component for this exercise can be accessed by clicking on the audio icon above (e-book), or by accessing the video 'Higher Music Literacy exercise 2' on the jm-education YouTube channel at *www.youtube/jm-education*. Answers are on page 134.

Exercise 2

This question is based on an arrangement of Irish folk music.

Listen to the excerpt and follow the guide to the music on the next page.

Here is the music for the first time.

You now have two minutes to read the question.

All answers must be written in (or below) the boxes on the next page.

(a) Insert the time signature in the correct place in the box.

(b) Describe the interval formed by the two notes in the box between **bar 3** and **bar 4**. Write your answer on the line below the box.

(c) Correct the rhythm in **bar 6** to match what you hear. Use the given blank bar.

(d) Insert the missing notes on the blank bar in **bar 9**. The rhythm is given.

(e) Transpose **bar 13 one octave lower** into the bass clef. Use the given blank bar.

(f) Identify the 3 bracketed notes in **bar 17** and **bar 18** as **Tonic**, **Subdominant** or **Dominant** notes. The key is E minor. Use the letters 'T' to indicate Tonic, 'S' for Subdominant and 'D' for dominant. Write your answers on the lines below each note in the box.

During the next three playings complete your answers (a) to (f).

The music will be played **three** more times with a pause of 30 seconds between playings and two minutes at the end to complete your answer.

Here is the music for the second time.

Here is the music for the third time.

Here is the music for the fourth time.

Chapter 3 Specimen Question Paper

 Listen in

www.youtube/jm-education

The audio component of this question paper is contained on the video, *Higher Music specimen question paper*, which can be accessed by clicking the audio icon above (e-book), or on the jm-education YouTube channel at *www.youtube/jm-education*. Answers are on pages 134–137.

 Take Note

In this examination you will listen to excerpts of music and answer questions on what you hear. The text of each question is printed on the question paper so that you can follow what the speaker says on the video. Listen carefully to the questions and to the music excerpts.

Some excerpts are played more than once. The number of times an excerpt will be played is stated in each question.

Write your answers in the spaces provided on the question paper or a printed copy of it, or on blank paper.

Attempt **ALL** questions.

The number of marks allocated to each question is indicated in the margin, with a total of **40 marks** available for the whole question paper.

The paper lasts **one hour**.

MARKS

Higher Music Specimen Question Paper

Total marks - ~~40~~ 31

Attempt ALL questions

Question 1

This question features instrumental music.

(a) Listen to this excerpt and identify **three** concepts in the music from those listed below. Read through the concepts before hearing the music.

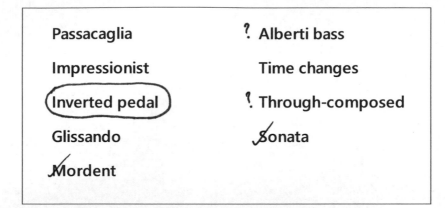

Passacaglia	? Alberti bass
Impressionist	Time changes
(Inverted pedal)	? Through-composed
Glissando	✓Sonata
✓Mordent	

Insert your **three** answers on the lines below.   ~~3~~
                                                                                    2

Mordent ✓

Sonata ✓

Through-composed

The music will be played **twice** with a pause of 10 seconds between playings and a pause of 40 seconds before question 1(b) starts.

Here is the music for the first time.
Here is the music for the second time.

(b) This question features vocal music. Name the concept which describes the vocal technique. The music will be played **once**.   ①

Coloratura ✓

Question 2   MARKS

This question features instrumental music.

A guide to the music is shown below. You are required to complete this guide by inserting music concepts.

There will now be a pause of 30 seconds to allow you to read through the question.

The music will be played **three** times, with a pause of 20 seconds between playings. You will then have a further 30 seconds to complete your answer.

In the first two playings, a voice will help guide you through the music. There is no voice in the third playing.

Here is the music for the first time.
Here is the music for the second time.
Here is the music for the third time

1	The melody features an ascending _Major_ ✓ _____ scale.	①
2	The playing technique used by the orchestral strings here is _pizzicato_ ✓ _____ (Italian term).	①
3	The instrument playing the melody is a/an _classical guitar_ ✓ _____.	①
4	The ornament here is a/an _trill_ ✓ _____.	①
5	The style of this type of instrumental work is known as a/an _concerto_ ✓ _____.	①

Question 3   MARKS

This question features music in contrasting styles.

Each excerpt will be played **once**.

(a) Listen to this excerpt and identify the style of the music.   ①

  impressionist ✓

(b) Listen to a different excerpt and describe the time signature.   ①

  compound   time ✓

(c) Listen to a new excerpt and identify the style of the music.   ✗

  Soul music   Jazz funk

Question 4   **MARKS**

This question is based on an arrangement of traditional Scottish music.

Listen to the excerpt and follow the guide to the music on the next page.

Here is the music for the first time.

You now have two minutes to read the question.

All answers must be written in or below the boxes on the next page.

(a) Insert the time signature in the correct place in the box .

(b) Transpose the notes in bar 4 **one octave lower** into the bass clef. Use the given blank bar.

(c) Correct the rhythm in **bar 7** to match what you hear. Write your answer in the box.

(d) What is the name given to the line between the two notes in **bar 11**? Write your answer on the line below the box.

(e) Complete the first four notes in **bar 13**. The rhythm is given.

(f) Describe the interval formed by the two notes in the box in **bar 16**. Write your answer on the line below the box. ①

During the next three playings complete your answers (a) to (f).

The music will be played **three** more times with a pause of 30 seconds between playings and a pause of 2 minutes before the next question starts.

Here is the music for the second time.

Here is the music for the third time.

Here is the music for the fourth time.

Question 4 Continued

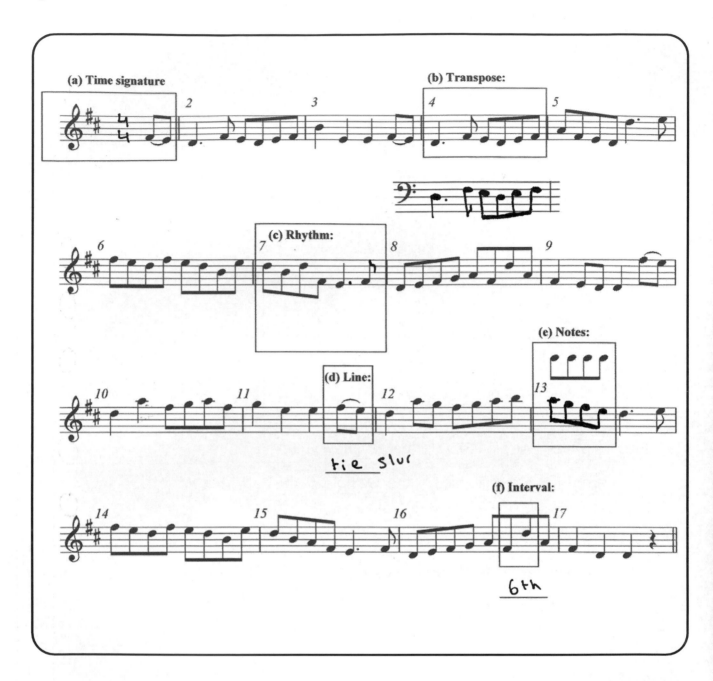

Question 5   MARKS

This question features instrumental music.

(a) Listen to this excerpt and identify **four** concepts in the music from those listed below. Read through the concepts before hearing the music.

Passacaglia	✓Tremolando/tremolo
Ritornello	Musique concrète
✓String quartet	Diminution
Obbligato	✓Pizzicato
Perfect cadence	? Irregular time signatures

Insert your **four** answers on the lines below.   ④

Pizzicato

Irregular time signatures

Tremolando

String quartet

The music will be played **three** times with a pause of 10 seconds between playings and a pause of 40 seconds before the next question starts.

Here is the music for the first time.
Here is the music for the second time.
Here is the music for the third time.

(b) Listen to this excerpt and identify the type of chord being played by the piano. The music will be played **once**.   ①

diminished 7th

(c) Listen to the following excerpt of vocal music and tick **one** box to describe what you hear. The music will be played **twice**.   ✗

☑ Lied
☑ Augmentation
☐ Coloratura
☐ Jazz-funk

Here is the music for the first time.
Here is the music for the second time.

49

Question 6   MARKS

This question is based on an excerpt of instrumental music.
In this question you should identify the most prominent concepts in the music.

As you listen, identify at least **two** concepts from each of the following headings:

Melody / Harmony   **Rhythm (Texture) / Tempo**   **Timbre / Dynamics**

You will hear the music **three times** and you should make notes as you listen.

Rough work will not be marked.

Marks will only be awarded for the final answer. After the third playing you will have three
minutes to write your final answer in the space provided on the next page.

  Here is the music for the first time.
  Here is the music for the second time.
  Here is the music for the third time.

6
5

Rough Work

Melody / Harmony	trill sequence perfect cadence Major relative minor
Rhythm (Texture) / Tempo	$\frac{3}{4}$ moderato homophonic
Timbre / Dynamics	strings celo diminuendo harpsichord forte - mezzo piano

Question 6 (continued)   MARKS

Final Answer

- Trill
- Perfect cadence
- starts major – modulates to relative minor

- $\frac{3}{4}$ timing, moderato tempo allegro
- homophonic texture

- Strings, celo (string quartet)
- harpsicord
- mezzo-forte – diminuendos to piano

Question 7   MARKS

This question is about comparing two excerpts of music.

Identify concepts present in each excerpt and then decide which **five** concepts are common to both excerpts. Both excerpts will be played **three** times with a pause of 10 seconds between playings.

As you listen, tick boxes in **Column A** and **Column B** to identify what you hear in Excerpt 1 and Excerpt 2.

These columns are for rough work only and will not be marked.

After the **three** playings of the music you will be given 2 minutes to decide which concepts are common to both excerpts and to tick **five** boxes in **Column C**.

You now have 1 minute to read through the question.

Here is Excerpt 1 for the first time. **Remember to tick concepts in Column A.**
Here is Excerpt 2 for the first time. **Remember to tick concepts in Column B.**

Here is Excerpt 1 for the second time.
Here is Excerpt 2 for the second time.

Here is Excerpt 1 for the third time.
Here is Excerpt 2 for the third time.

You now have 2 minutes to identify the **five** concepts common to both excerpts.

Remember to tick five boxes only in Column C.

3

Question 7 (continued)   MARKS

Concepts		Column A Excerpt 1	Column B Excerpt 2	Column C 5 features common to both
Melody/Harmony	Ascending major scale	✓	✓	✓ ✓
	Interrupted cadence			
	Glissando			
	Key change			✓
Timbre	Harmonics			
	Woodwind solo	✓	✓	✓ ✓
	Timpani	✓.	✓.	✓ ✓
Texture/ Structure / Form	Rondo			
	Through-composed	?✓	?.	✓
	Theme and variation			
Style	Impressionist	✗ ✓	?.	✓
	Symphony			✓
	Concerto			
			5 marks	3

Question 8   **MARKS**

This question is based on an excerpt from a modern peace song.

Below is a list of features which occur in the music.

There will now be a pause of 1 minute to allow you to read through the question.

The lyrics of the song are printed in the table on the following page. You should insert each feature **once** in the column on the right at the point where it occurs.

You only need to insert the **bold** words on the question paper.

- Piano accompaniment plays a short solo passage of <u>**syncopated**</u> music

- Piano accompaniment texture changes from arpeggios to <u>**chords**</u>

- Vocal <u>**crescendo**</u> reaches its loudest volume

- After a key modulation, the music returns to the original <u>**key**</u> heard at the start of the excerpt

- Lead vocalist and backing vocalist sing 'Shine on' in <u>**unison**</u> two consecutive times

The music will now be played **three** times with a pause of 20 seconds between playings and a pause of 30 seconds at the end.

Here is the music for the first time.

Here is the music for the second time.

Here is the music for the third time

Question 8 (continued) MARKS

- Piano accompaniment plays a short solo passage of **syncopated** music   *Syn*

- Piano accompaniment texture changes from arpeggios to **chords**   *Cho*

- Vocal **crescendo** reaches its loudest volume   *cresc*

- After a key modulation, the music returns to the original **key** heard at the start of the excerpt   *Key*

- Lead vocalist and backing vocalist sing 'Shine on' in **unison** two consecutive times   *uni*

5/3

Shine on, through the dark, shine on	1		
Shine on, shine on...	2	*✓*	*syn*
We all pass through this world of changes	3	*Syncopated chords*	*Sync*
In a blink of forever's eye	4		
But on the path of wisdom	5		
We learn that nothing ever really dies	6	*crescendo ✓*	*cres*
Shine on, in a new life, shine on	7	*chords Key*	*cho*
Shine on, perfect star, shine on	8		
Shine on, share the light, shine on	9		
Shine on, shine on, shine on	10	*unison ✓*	*u*
Shine on, share the light	11	*Key*	*k*
Shine on, always bright, shine on	12		

Chapter 4 Composing Workshop: Scots Song

For information on the requirements and assessment procedure for the composing element of Higher Music see *Composing assignment* on page v.

This chapter is a workshop in which you will be taken through the compositional processes used to create a vocal piece which gets its 'Scottish sound' from the use of **modal** scales, giving it the character of a traditional **folk song** (many of which are **modal**).

You have the option to compose your own piece step-by-step (recommended) as you go through each part of the workshop, or just absorb the effective techniques used and try them later in your composing activities.

Although I will not be adding lyrics to the piece written in the workshop (I'm leaving this as an optional practice exercise for you), you can of course do so in your own song, either when the **melody** is completed or while you are composing it.

Alternatively, you might choose to compose music to fit existing words – taken from a poem, for example.

We will begin by composing the **melody** one step at a time, paying attention to particular musical elements (concepts) which can provide the piece with its Scottish character, and then add a **piano accompaniment**. The finished song for **solo voice** and **piano** can also be heard when later arranged as an instrumental piece using a Digital Audio Workstation (DAW) (pages 84-86).

 Take Note

Using improvisation and/or musical loops in your composition

There are very specific guidelines on the use of improvisation and pre-recorded sound loops in the Higher Music course, should you wish to use either (or both) of these in the music you submit for the composing assignment.

Improvisation may be used in sections of your piece, but only as part of a larger composition which shows clear composing skills. A piece of music which uses only improvisation is not acceptable.

Pre-recorded sound loops can be included in your piece, but these must be used in a creative way that demonstrates a compositional process resulting in a coherent and structured piece of music.

The Seven Basic Modes

Before we start composing, let's review **modal** music.

Modes date back to medieval times before music notation as we know it today was developed. Although the names of the modes can sound a bit complex, **modal** music is actually very simple to understand.

If you choose a **D** note on a **keyboard** instrument and then play only the successive *white keys* up (or down) to the next **D** (one **octave**), this is the *Dorian* mode. Do the same thing starting on an **F** note and you will play the *Lydian* mode. It's that simple! Every **modal scale** has a unique sound because a different order of **tones** and **semitones** occurs in each **mode**.

Mode names and their 'home' notes

This mode	Begins on this note
Ionian	C
Dorian	D
Phrygian	E
Lydian	F
Mixolydian	G
Aeolian	A
Locrian	B

The starting note of a **mode** can be considered the 'home' note to which, much like a **key** note in **tonal** music, you would return whenever you wanted to create a phrase ending – as in a **perfect cadence**.

Great advice... **Top Tip**

To help you remember the order of the modes (beginning with **C**; the Ionian **mode**), you might find the following phrase a useful memory-jogger:

I	Don't	Pretend	Little	Monkeys	Are	Large
O	O	H	Y	I	E	O
N	R	R	D	X	O	C
I	I	Y	I	O	L	R
A	A	G	A	L	I	I
N	N	I	N	Y	A	A
		A		D	N	N
		N		I		
				A		
				N		

Chords built from Modal Scales

Since the order of **tones** and **semitones** changes in each **modal scale**, it follows that the ordering of **chords** (whether **major** or **minor**) built from the notes in these **scales** will also be variable. For example, the **chord** built from the first note of the *Ionian* mode (**C**) is a **major chord**, whereas in the *Dorian* **mode** (beginning on **D**) the first **chord** is **minor**.

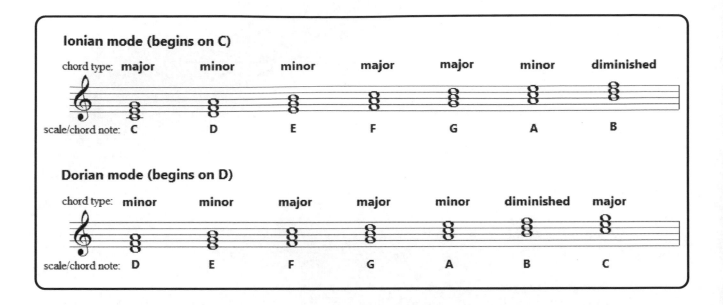

Important points about modal music

- No **key signatures** are used in the seven *basic* **modes**, but **accidentals** (**sharps** and **flats**) can be used to add 'colour' or **chromaticism** in a piece of **modal** music, and at **cadences** where the 7th note of the **mode** is often sharpened to create a smooth **perfect cadence**.

- **Harmony** is generally much simpler in **modal** music than it is in **tonal** music, with less variety of **chords** and fewer **chord** inversions used (see *Clever chord inversions*, page 75). This helps to maintain the simplicity and specific character of the **modal** sound.

- The **chords** chosen to harmonise a **modal melody** can greatly strengthen the **modal** sound. For example, the **chords** built from the *second* and *third* notes of a **modal scale** are often used freely for their particular sound, whereas in classical music these **chords** (**II** and **III**) are used rather less frequently, perhaps only appearing as part of very specific **chord progressions** (such as **II-V-I**).

- Other types of modes known as 'altered modes' exist. These are **modes** which have certain notes altered to make specific sounds and are most commonly used in modern popular styles such as **rock** music.

Using keys with modal music

Although basic modes do not have **key signatures**, modes can still be used in music which has a **key**. If you think of each **mode** as representing the seven different notes of a **scale**, you can easily play any **mode** in any **key**. For example, consider that each mode is numbered from 1 to 7...

1. **Ionian**	5. **Mixolydian**
2. **Dorian**	6. **Aeolian**
3. **Phrygian**	7. **Locrian**
4. **Lydian**	

The number of each **mode** corresponds to the same note number of a **scale**. So, if you are in the key of **F major** and choose the *fourth* note of that **scale** (**B flat**) as your 'key note' instead of **F**, you will create the *Lydian* **mode**. Choose the third note of the same **scale** (**A**) as the 'key note' and you will now get the *phrygian* **mode**.

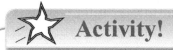
Activity!

Try experimenting with the sounds of different **modes** in a variety of **keys** by first of all selecting a **key**, then working your way up through the **modes** from *Ionian* to *Locrian*, choosing each note of the **scale** (1-7) as a new 'key note'.

Step 1: The plan for 'Scots Song'

When composing most types of songs you can either write music to existing lyrics (which you may have written yourself), or compose the music first and then add lyrics to suit the notes and **rhythm**. Sometimes it can be a combination of both methods, and the piece will grow from a number of musical and lyrical ideas. In my *Scots song* I am going to concentrate on the **melody** and **piano accompaniment** and leave the lyrics to *you*!

To add a little more interest to my song, I have chosen not to take the more traditional approach of writing clearly defined **verse** and **chorus** sections (although you can do so if you wish), but instead base the song on three different melodic ideas – or **themes** as I will be calling them. The themes will contrast slightly with each other but still be related through certain common **rhythms** and note patterns, with parts being **repeated**, sometimes with **variation**, throughout the piece. The aim of this type of plan is to produce a less formal or 'looser' structure which sounds slightly more **through-composed** than would be the case had I chosen a **verse-chorus-verse** formula.

To begin, remember that it is very helpful to jot down all your ideas – including the musical elements or concepts you think will help to create the right **style** and mood – followed by a basic structure plan. You don't need to stick rigidly to this plan, of course, but even working loosely within a certain structure can ensure that your final piece will be well-balanced.

Here are my own ideas and structure plan:

Elements which will help to create a 'Scottish' sound

- **Scotch snaps**

- **Dotted rhythms** (these are a feature of the **Strathspey**, for example)

- **Modal** and/or **pentatonic** scales

- Fairly simple **chords/harmony** (with **chords II** and **III** used for their **modal** sound)

- Instruments: **voice** with **piano accompaniment** (which could be extended or arranged to include **folk** instruments such as **fiddle**, **whistle**, and **clarsach**)

Other useful compositional elements

- **4-bar piano introduction**

- **Through-composed** or less formal structure

- Recurring melodic **theme** (functioning as a kind of **chorus**), but varied on each repeat

- **Instrumental** section

- Simple but memorable musical phrases

- **Anacrusis**

Structure Plan

SECTION	A	B	A1
4-bar piano introduction	Theme 1 Ionian mode 'major' sound (use major chords)	Theme 2 (contrast) 'minor' sound (add minor chords)	First repeat of Theme 1 with some slight variation
4 bars	4-8 bars	4-8 bars	4-8 bars
C	**A2**	**D**	**A3**
Theme 3 (change mode for contrast) 'minor' sound (use different minor chords from those used in Theme 2)	Second repeat of Theme 1 with a new kind of variation	Piano instrumental based on Section C (Theme 3) or previously-heard melodic fragments	Coda consisting of a final varied repeat of Theme 1 (perhaps with a metre change)
4-8 bars	4-8 bars	4-8 bars	4-8 bars

 Take Note

Notice the similarity between the planned structure for my **song** and **rondo** form. Most songs have a kind of **rondo** structure where the **chorus** can be regarded as the recurring '**A**' section and the **verses** the contrasting **episodes** (**B**, **C** and **D** sections).

 Activity!

Plan and listen

Start off your own song now by making a list of the musical elements or concepts that you think will be effective in the piece, followed by a structure plan sketch. When working out your plan, remember that **songs** and **ballads** normally have **verses** (where the lyrics change with each new **verse**) and **choruses** (where the lyrics are normally the same each time), but you can also choose a looser, more varied style as I have. Before you begin your song it would be helpful to listen to a few **Scottish songs/ballads** for some inspiration and structural guidelines.

Step 2: Composing Section A (Theme 1)

Although I want to begin my song with a **4-bar piano introduction**, I will not write this until the rest of the piece has been composed since the completed song will help to determine the music of the introduction.

The **style** of this piece dictates that the music should be kept fairly simple, with no overly-complicated vocal passages or complex **accompaniment**, but that doesn't mean we can't write a really good, atmospheric and memorable **melody** – the kind you might find yourself whistling or humming spontaneously while walking down the street! So the aim is to make every note matter, whilst keeping everything reasonably uncomplicated.

A comfortable **vocal range** is from about **middle C** to the **C** an **octave** above it.

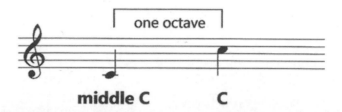

Of course, it is possible to sing notes much higher and lower than this, depending on the skill of the singer and whether the voice is male or female (I have a **soprano** voice in mind for my **song**, so I can go a bit higher), but keeping within a certain **range** means that more people will be able to sing the music you compose.

I have chosen to build my **song** from the basic *Ionian* **mode**, which begins on the note **C**. Written below are the seven main **chords** of this **mode**; these will help me to compose the **song** since I can use **chord notes** to construct parts of my **melody**, or let the sound of certain **chord progressions** influence each new **theme** I write.

Chords in the Ionian Mode

Mode note	C	D	E	F	G	A	B
Chord	C major	D minor	E minor	F major	G major	A minor	B diminished
	(I)	(II)	(III)	(IV)	(V)	(VI)	(VII)

Take Note

You will see that the notes and **chords** of the *Ionian* **mode** are the same as those found in the **key** of **C major**. That is because in each case there are no **sharps** or **flats (accidentals)** used. In all other **modes** the difference in the sound is more obvious. For example, the basic *Dorian* **mode** (which would begin on the second note (**D**) in the example on the previous page) doesn't have the **F#** and **C#** found in the **key** of **D major**, or the **Bb** and **C#** found in the **key** of **D minor**.

I had no melodic ideas in my head for the song when I began, so, in order to generate something, I started improvising with the *Ionian* **mode** and the **C pentatonic major scale** (the notes of which are found in the *Ionian* **mode**). I also experimented with the individual notes of the **chords** in the *Ionian* **mode**, whilst incorporating **dotted rhythms** and **Scotch snaps**, and soon came up with a 4-bar phrase I liked (see below.) Note the **chords** written above the music which helped to influence the **melody** notes.

First 4-bar phrase

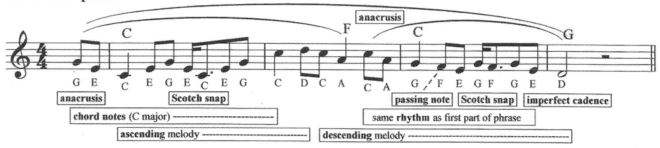

The 4-bar **phrase** is made up of two smaller phrases (indicated by the two **phrase marks** underneath the longer single **phrase mark**) which have an almost identical **rhythm** and use **anacrusis** and **Scotch snaps**. (Notice also how this opening **phrase** makes use of **chord notes** and a **passing note**).

The full phrase finishes on the note **D**, forming an **imperfect cadence**. Had I wanted to end more decisively I could have chosen a note here that would fit with the **chord** of **C major** in order to make a **perfect cadence**.

 **Listen in**

Excerpt 1. First 4-bar phrase

You can hear the opening 4-bar phrase by clicking on the audio icon above (e-book), or accessing the YouTube video, '**Composing Workshop: excerpts for Scots Song**' (Excerpt 1 at *01.02*) on the jm-education YouTube channel at ***www.youtube/jm-education***.

All of the elements used for this opening phrase are going to be important in the construction of the rest of the **song**.

The effect of the **imperfect cadence** at the end of my first **phrase** has been to create a **Question** which needs an **Answer** to balance it out and so complete a larger section of music. This section will be the first **theme** of my song as outlined in the structure plan.

Having already established the song's character and central musical elements in the opening 4-bar **Question** phrase, I used these to guide me as I composed the **Answer** phrase – the natural flow of which seemed to move *down* towards the note **C** and a **perfect cadence**.

Excerpt 2. Theme 1

Below are the **Question** and **Answer** phrases which make up **Theme 1** of my song. Follow the notation as you listen to excerpt 2 by clicking on the audio icon above (e-book), or accessing the YouTube video, **'Composing Workshop: excerpts for Scots Song'** (Excerpt 2 at *01.20*) on the jm-education YouTube channel at *www.youtube/jm-education*.

SECTION A   **(Theme 1)**

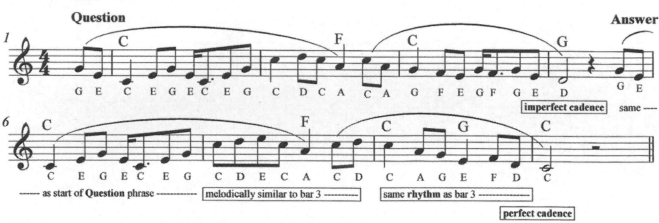

Features of *contrast* in the **Answer** phrase:

- Bars 7,8 and 9 are original music
- The **Answer** phrase ends with a **perfect cadence** in bar 9

Features of *unity* in the **Question** and **Answer** phrases:

- The first part of the **Answer** phrase (end of bar 5 and all of bar 6) is the same as the start of the **Question** phrase (end of bar 1 and all of bar 2)
- The second full bar of the **Answer** phrase (bar 7) has some **melodic** similarity to the second full bar of the **Question** phrase (bar 3)

Activity!

Your Turn...

Following the plan for your own song (and using my opening **theme** as a guide) compose a melodic **theme** or a **verse** which has a strong Scottish feel to it, bearing in mind the musical elements which can help you to achieve this, such as **Scotch snaps**, **dotted rhythms** and **modal** or **pentatonic scales**. Just start experimenting and see what kind of 'tunes' begin to develop!

Once you have completed the music of your opening **verse** or **theme** you might want to **repeat** it again (perhaps with some **variation**) and make this extended **melody** the first section of your song. Doing that would of course expand your finished piece further, but remember, the most important thing is that the music 'feels' right when you hear it, so always let your instinct guide you.

Step 3: Composing Section B (Theme 2)

For *contrast* in my second theme I am going to raise the **pitch** of the notes a little, and also create a slightly darker sound in places by using **melody** notes taken from **minor chords** found in the *Ionian* **mode**. To maintain a sense of *unity* I will include **Scotch snaps** and **anacrusis**, and keep the same kind of 2-bar phrase structure used in the first **theme**.

Here are the various points I noted down before composing the second **theme**:

Contrast:
- Create a darker sound by building parts of the **melody** from **minor chords** used in the *Ionian* **mode**
- Raise the **pitch** of the **melody** slightly

Unity:
- Keep using **Scotch snaps**
- Keep using **anacrusis**
- Add some fragments of the **melody** used in the first **theme**, but **vary** these – perhaps by altering the **rhythm** or adding some new notes

 **Listen in**

Excerpt 3. Theme 2

Below is the music of my second **theme** which you can follow as you listen to excerpt 3 by clicking on the audio icon above (e-book), or accessing the YouTube video, '**Composing Workshop: excerpts for Scots Song**' (Excerpt 3 at *01.50*) on the jm-education YouTube channel at *www.youtube/jm-education*.

SECTION [B] **(Theme 2)**

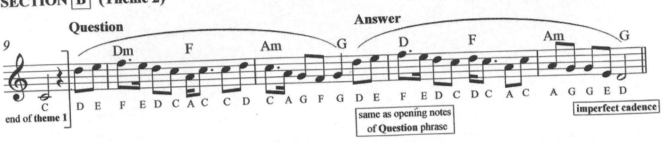

You will see that the second **theme** is just four bars long. The single 4-bar phrase sounded effective when played after the music of the first **theme**, so I was happy to make this alteration to the 4-bar **Question** phrase/4-bar **Answer** phrase structure of **theme 1** – which in itself provides an element of **variation**. The second **theme** still has **Question** and **Answer** phrases, but these are each just two bars long instead of four.

According to plan, though, I have raised the **pitch** of the **melody** and added some 'darker' **minor chords** for *contrast* whilst maintaining *unity* through the **rhythm**, **Scotch snaps** and **anacrusis**. Notice also how I have incorporated **passing notes** between the **chord notes**.

The second **theme** ends on the note **D** (from the **chord of G major**), making an **imperfect cadence** which will lead the music nicely into the first **repeat** of **theme 1**.

 **Activity!**

Write the next part of your song now (which in your case might be a **chorus** or a new **theme**), keeping in mind the techniques I have just used in my own piece to create both *contrast* and *unity* whilst still preserving the basic simplicity of the **melody**.

Step 4: Composing Section A1 (Theme 1 repeated with some variation)

The next part of the structure plan for my song involves **repeating** theme 1 with a little **variation** added to it. Here are some **variation** techniques which might be used in a **repeated** section of music:

- Add some new **melodic** material in between bars of **repeated** music
- Change one or two notes in a bar
- Create a new **rhythm** for parts of the **repeated** music
- Create a new **melody** for a **rhythm** which is being **repeated**
- Reduce/increase the length of the **repeated** section
- **Repeat** note passages in **augmentation** or **diminution**

 **Listen in**

Excerpt 4. Theme 1 varied

Below is my music for the **varied repeat** of **theme 1**, which you can follow as you listen to excerpt 4 by clicking on the audio icon above (e-book), or accessing the YouTube video, '**Composing Workshop: excerpts for Scots Song**' (Excerpt 4 at *02.08*) on the jm-education YouTube channel at ***www.youtube/jm-education***. Compare it with the original version of **Theme 1** on page 64 (Excerpt 2 at *01.20*).

SECTION A1 (varied repeat of Theme 1)

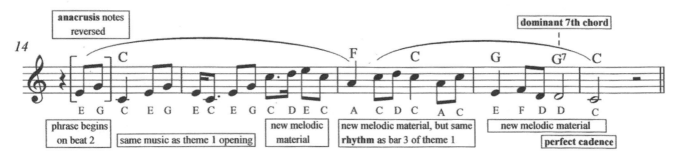

You will see that again I have used just a single 4-bar phrase for this section, shortening the **repeat** of the first **theme** by half and finishing with a **perfect cadence**. I have also rearranged the music so that the notes now fall on *different beats of the bar* to those of the original first **theme**: the **anacrusis** at the start of the **repeat** of **theme 1**, for example, now begins on beat *two* of the bar as opposed to beat *four*. This 'displaces' all the beats of the music which follows. You might think that doing this would have upset the overall symmetry of the piece, but in fact the result is quite effective, and has produced a nice element of **variation**.

Also for **variation** I reversed the order of the opening **anacrusis** notes and inserted some new **melodic** material in bars 15, 16 and 17, whereas a sense of *unity* is maintained by **repeating** certain notes and **rhythms** from the original **theme 1**.

 **Activity!**

Depending on the structure you have chosen for your song, at this stage you will be either repeating the first **theme** (like me) or writing a second **verse** (this could be a varied **repeat** of your first **verse**). If you are repeating **theme 1**, consider the possibility of adding some **variation** (which may simply involve reducing the length of the section), but you may ultimately feel that an *identical* **repeat** is the preferable option. Whatever you choose, the last three composing steps should be a helpful guide to you.

Step 5: Composing Section C (Theme 3)

Now it's time to write the next section of new music for my song, the third **theme**. As before, the main aim will be to create *contrast* here for **melodic** interest whilst still preserving the basic *unity*, simplicity and flow overall.

Here is the list of ideas I had for achieving both *contrast* and *unity* in the new theme:

Contrast:
- Base the new **theme** on the *Aeolian* **mode** (**minor** sound) to create a **modulation**, but return to the original *Ionian* **mode** (**major** sound) again at the end since the next section (the second **repeat** of **theme 1**) will be in this **mode**
- Add some new **rhythms**
- Alter the **rhythm** of the **anacrusis**

Unity:
- Maintain the same basic **rhythmic** flow and phrase structure as the previous sections of music
- Keep using **Scotch snaps**
- Use some **rhythms** and **melodic** fragments from previous sections of the piece

To spark off some ideas for this new **theme** I tried improvising with the *Aeolian* **mode** and the **A pentatonic minor scale**, as well as the **chords** of **A minor** and **E minor** (**chords I** and **V** of the *Aeolian* **mode**), whilst also incorporating my ideas for achieving *contrast* and *unity*.

Listen in

Excerpt 5. Theme 3

Working within these helpful and structured guidelines it wasn't long before I had composed my new **theme** (shown below). Study the music carefully before listening to excerpt 5 by clicking on the audio icon above (e-book), or accessing the YouTube video, '**Composing Workshop: excerpts for Scots Song**' (Excerpt 5 at *02.27*) on the jm-education YouTube channel at ***www.youtube/jm-education***.

Note the ways in which I have made use of the following:

- **Chord notes** (based on **arpeggios**)
- **Passing notes**
- *Aeolian* **mode/A pentatonic minor**
- New **rhythms**: **dotted crotchets** and **semiquavers**

- **Repeated rhythms**
- **Repeated bars**/note groups
- **Variation**
- **Scotch snaps**
- New **anacrusis rhythm**

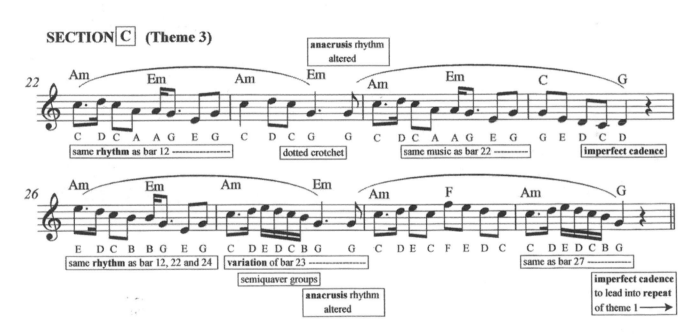

 Activity!

If you are writing your song with a traditional **verse-chorus-verse** structure, the next step for you will probably involve simply **repeating** the **chorus** that you have already composed. On the other hand, if you are following a similar structure to mine, then you will now need to compose a third contrasting **theme**, perhaps changing the **scale** or **mode** in order to create a **modulation**. Remember that by adding just a single new **rhythm** you can inject an element of **variation** into your music.

Step 6: Section A 2 (second repeat of Theme 1)

After playing all of the sections I had composed so far (in order), now seemed the right time to **repeat** all eight bars of **theme 1** (as opposed to reducing it to just four bars as I did in the first **repeat** of this **theme** at bar 14). I made just two small changes to the **theme** this time (see music below): the first was to add three new notes in bar 36 (the high **F** note adds a bit more drama as well as **variation**), the second involved tagging on an extra bar in **2/4 time** at the end. The **2/4 bar** is used to extend the end of the **theme** and create a little extra 'breathing space' before the next section, the **piano instrumental**, begins. Doing this also strengthens the suggestion that one section of music has finished and another new one is about to start.

Listen in

Excerpt 6. Theme 1 second repeat

While following the music below, listen to the second **repeat** of **Theme 1** by clicking on the audio icon above (e-book), or accessing the jm-education YouTube video, **'Composing Workshop: excerpts for Scots Song'** (Excerpt 6 at *02.57*) on the jm-education YouTube channel at: ***www.youtube/jm-education***.

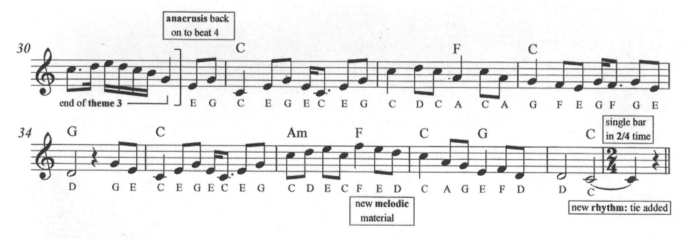

Activity!

Your own song will probably be repeating a **theme** or a **verse** now in which you might want to add some small (but effective) **variations** as I did in the second **repeat** of my first **theme**. The simple addition of an extra bar to create a smooth *link* into the next section of your piece might be all that's needed, or you could decide to do something a bit more creative, such as **modulate** into another **mode** or add some completely new **rhythms**. You might feel, however, that the best result will be achieved by simply **repeating** a previous **theme/verse** with no **variation** at all. Don't be tempted to add something different to your piece just for the sake of doing so; often the most straightforward option will produce the best musical effect, so don't try to be *too* clever!

Step 7: Section D (the piano instrumental)

Although the main role of the **piano** in my song is to provide an **accompaniment** (composed later in this workshop), in the **instrumental** section its function is also going to be **melodic**, where it will **repeat** the **melody** of **theme 3** (with the right hand), and accompany itself using **chords** (played by the left hand). Having an instrument **repeat** a phrase or a whole section of music which was previously sung (or played on a different instrument) is another effective composing technique which provides both *contrast* and *unity* – without the need to write any original material!

Since the **piano** will be simply **repeating** theme 3 without any **variation**, there is no need to give a musical example here, but you will see how this section (complete with **chord accompaniment**) fits with the rest of the music when the notation for the completed song is given on pages 80-82.

If the plan for your song includes an instrumental section, consider following my example by **repeating** music which was previously written for the vocal part, such as a **verse**, **theme** or **chorus**. Alternatively you could compose an instrumental which incorporates only *fragments* of the vocal **melody** used in other parts of the piece, or even write a completely original section of music.

As always, though, if you go for the more creative option of composing original music, be careful to ensure that it fits with the rest of the piece - as opposed to sounding like an unrelated section that has simply been stuck on!

Step 8: Composing Section A 3 The Coda (varied repeat of Theme 1)

To finish my **melody** I have chosen to write a **Coda** based on a **variation** of **theme 1**. However, if the ending is to stand out a bit more from the previous music, this time the **variation** technique will have to be different from any I have used so far.

In my structure plan I noted the possibility of changing the **metre** of the music here, which would mean that I could vary the original **theme** considerably without having to alter any of the notes. The first most obvious contrasting **metre** which came to mind was **triple metre**, so I tried playing **theme 1** in **3/4 time**, changing some of the **rhythms** and using **augmentation** in places where this felt right, and was pleased with the result straight away. The change of **metre**, combined with **augmentation**, had the effect of slowing down the **melody** a little without there actually being a reduction in **tempo**. This was a particularly effective kind of **variation** to have in my **Coda** - again achieved using composing techniques which allowed me to produce something new in the piece without actually having to write a whole new section of music.

71

 **Listen in**

Excerpt 7. Coda

Below is the music for my **Coda** which you can follow as you listen to excerpt 7 by clicking on the audio icon above (e-book), or accessing the jm-education YouTube video, **'Composing Workshop: excerpts for Scots Song'** (Excerpt 7 at *03.30*) on the jm-education YouTube channel at ***www.youtube/jm-education***. Afterwards, note the elements of *contrast* and *unity* I incorporated into this final section of my song (see below).

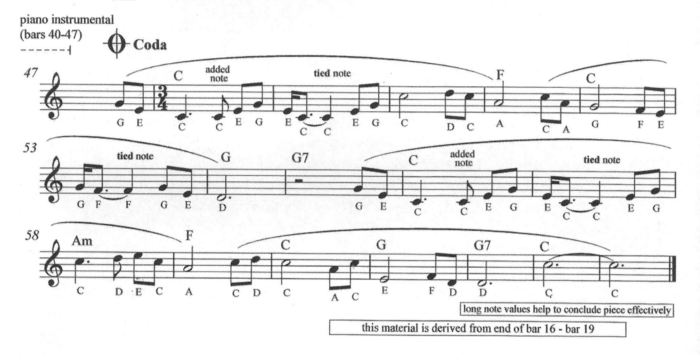

SECTION [A3] Coda (varied repeat of Theme 1)

Contrast:

- **Metre change** to **3/4 time**, meaning that most of the notes from **theme 1** now occur on a different beat of the bar than previously. (**Theme 1** was originally in **4/4 time**.)
- **Augmentation** used on some of the notes to extend their values: **dotted crotchets, ties** and **minims** are used for this purpose
- An extra note is added in bar **48**, and again in bar **56**

Unity:

- The **Coda** repeats most of the **melody** of **theme 1**, with only the last few bars altered to conclude the piece more emphatically.

 **Activity!**

For this final step in your song's **melody** you might be **repeating** the **chorus** with little or no **variation**, or you could make the last section an extended **Coda**, as I did, in order to create a more eventful ending. Think it over carefully, drawing upon the various ideas and techniques used so far in this workshop to guide you as you consider the options for making your song's conclusion a little different. Always be prepared to experiment, and remember to trust your instincts concerning what sounds good as opposed to doing something clever just for its own sake.

 Listen in

Excerpt 8. Completed melody

On page 74 is the completed **melody** of my *Scots song* showing the **chords** which helped to influence its construction and which will also be used to **harmonise** it when I write the **piano accompaniment** in step 9.

Follow the music as you listen to excerpt 8 by clicking on the audio icon above (e-book), or accessing the jm-education YouTube video, **'Composing Workshop: excerpts for Scots Song'** (Excerpt 8 at *04.18*) on the jm-education YouTube channel at *www.youtube/jm-education*.

Scots Song

Joe McGowan

Step 9. The piano accompaniment

As the **chords** that I will be using to compose the **piano accompaniment** are the same as those which helped me write the **melody**, all I really need to do now is think about *how* I am going to use these **chords** again to write a good **accompaniment**.

The relative simplicity of the song means that I don't want to write a complex **piano** part that will either interfere too much with the natural flow of the **melody** or conflict with the general **style** of the music. But that doesn't mean the **accompaniment** has to be bland...

Clever chord inversions

I am going to use **chord** inversions in my **piano accompaniment**. Put simply, this just involves moving the three notes within a basic **chord** (*triad*) around a little. **Chord** inversions are a fantastic way to create new sounds from the same **chord**, thereby adding interest or 'colour' to bars where the same **chord** is used throughout or **bass** lines are sounding too static.

Here's how they work:

- **Root position**: A basic **chord** is constructed from a **root** note with the **intervals** a **3rd** and a **5th** higher than that **root** note stacked on top. (see examples on pages 31 and 32). So, the **chord** of **C major** is formed with the notes **C** (**root** note), **E** (a **3rd** higher than **C**), and **G** (a **5th** higher than **C**). This is known as a **chord** in *root position*.

- **First inversion**: If we replace the **root** note (**C**) with the note a **3rd** higher (**E**) so that it is now the lowest note in the **chord**, we have a **chord** in *first inversion* (see below).

- **Second inversion**: If we replace the **root** note (**C**) with the note a **5th** higher (**G**) so that it is now the lowest note in the **chord**, we have a **chord** in *second inversion* (see below).

Note: The lowest note in a **chord** (or in the **bass** part) always determines the *position* of that **chord** – i.e. *root position*, *first inversion* or *second inversion*.

Chord of C major in *Root position, First inversion* **and** *Second inversion*

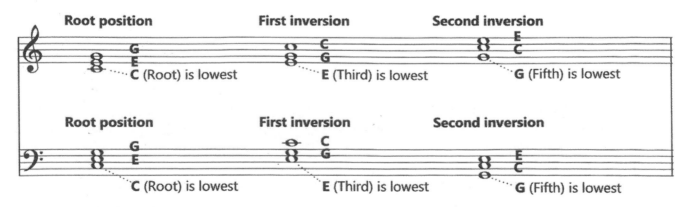

Chord abbreviations

- **Root position chords are indicated by Roman numbers: I, II, III, IV, V, VI, VII**

Roman numbers (**I**, **II**, **IV**, **V** etc.) describe which **chord** (**Tonic**, **Subdominant**, **Dominant** etc.) from a particular **key** or **mode** is being used in *root* position - e.g. **C major**, **D minor**, **F major**.

- **First inversion chords are indicated by the letter 'b' after the Roman number: Ib, IIb, IIIb, IVb, Vb, VIb, VIIb**

A *first inversion* **chord** is abbreviated to a Roman number followed by the letter 'b'. Therefore, Ib is used for the **tonic chord** in its *first inversion*. For example, in the **key** of **C major**, Ib would indicate **chord I** (**C major**) in its *first inversion* (where the note **E** is now the lowest note in the **chord** (<u>E</u> G C rather than <u>C</u> E G)).

IVb therefore describes the **Subdominant chord** in its *first inversion*. In the key of **C major** this would be an **F major chord** (**chord IV**) with the note **A** as the lowest note in the **chord** (<u>A</u> C F rather than <u>F</u> A C).

- **Second inversion chords are indicated by the letter 'c' after the Roman number: Ic, IIc, IIIc, IVc, Vc, VIc, VIIc,**

A *second inversion* **chord** is abbreviated to a Roman number followed by the letter 'c'. So, Ic is used for the **tonic chord** in its *second inversion*. In the **key** of **C major**, Ic would therefore indicate **chord I** (**C major**) in its *second inversion* (where the note **G** is now the lowest note in the **chord** (<u>G</u> C E rather than <u>C</u> E G)).

Vc then describes the **Dominant chord** in its *second inversion*. In the **key** of **C major** this would be a **G major chord** (**chord V**) with the note **D** as the lowest note in the **chord** (<u>D</u> G B rather than <u>G</u> B D).

Note: You can see **chords** being abbreviated in this way on the score of *Scots Song* on pages 80-82.

 Activity!

If you haven't already decided on the **chords** you will be using to **harmonise** your song, do this now. Experiment with all the **chords** in the **mode**(s) or **key**(s) you have used, but keep the **accompaniment** uncomplicated – and don't forget that **chords II** and **III** can be incorporated freely in **modal harmony**. You might also want to experiment with some **chord** inversions.

When I was experimenting with various **accompaniment** styles and **chord** inversions it became obvious that the more basic techniques were indeed the most effective in this piece, and anything which was too busy (or clever!) could easily disturb the all-important flow of the **melody**. Even those **chords** I tried which contained more than the three notes of a basic *triad* often sounded a little too powerful, so I eventually settled for a straightforward but effective **piano accompaniment** style where the right hand plays the *triad* and the left hand has a single-note **bass** line. This style ensures that the **harmony** is clear in every bar whilst none of the **chords** overpower the **melody**, and the **accompaniment** in general remains uncomplicated.

I also wanted to avoid having similar **rhythms** between the **melody** and **piano accompaniment**, so I introduced a **dotted crotchet** and **quaver rhythm** into the **accompaniment**, which provided *contrast* with the vocal **melody** without interfering with it.

 **Listen in**

Excerpt 9. First 5 bars accompanied

Below are the first five bars of the **melody** for '*Scots Song*', complete with **piano accompaniment**, which you can follow as you listen to excerpt 9 by clicking on the audio icon above (e-book), or accessing the jm-education YouTube video, **'Composing Workshop: excerpts for Scots Song'** (Excerpt 9 at *07.13*) on the jm-education YouTube channel at ***www.youtube/jm-education***. The **accompanied** version of the whole song can be found on pages 80-82).

First five bars of *Scots Song* **melody with piano accompaniment**

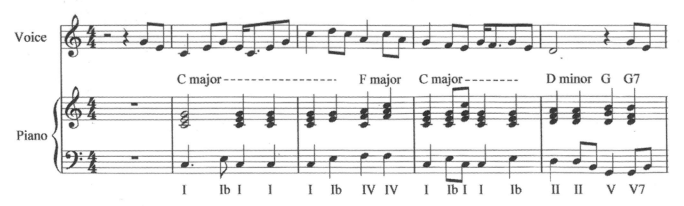

There are two places in my song where I alter this style of **accompaniment**: the **piano** instrumental section and the **Coda**. In the **piano** instrumental you will remember that the right hand plays the **melody**, so I had to 'switch' the **chords** from right hand to left hand here, and in the **Coda** I have *both* hands playing chords in certain places; this adds power to the section and helps reinforce the effect of the music reaching its conclusion.

Other features of my **piano accompaniment** include **passing notes** and **contrary motion**, and there are one or two areas where the **bass** part (left hand) *answers* the **melody** or *imitates* a **melodic rhythm** used earlier in the piece. All of these features in the **accompaniment** can be seen on the score of '*Scots Song*' on pages 80–82.

Step 10. The piano introduction

To complete '*Scots Song*' all that remained for me now was to write the 4-bar **piano** introduction.

As I predicted in the early stages of this workshop, leaving the introduction to last made the task easier since I was able to draw upon various musical features already used in the piece to compose an introduction which sounded balanced with the rest of the music.

I based the 4-bar **piano** introduction on a straightforward **descending** phrase which uses **anacrusis**, **Scotch snap**, and **dotted crotchet** notes in its construction, as well as simple *triads* (3-note chords) in the left hand part.

 **Listen in**

Excerpt 10. Piano introduction

You can hear the **piano** Introduction by clicking on the audio icon above (e-book), or accessing the jm-education YouTube video, **'Composing Workshop: excerpts for Scots Song'** (Excerpt 10 at *07.35*) on the jm-education YouTube channel at *www.youtube/jm-education*. The music is shown below.

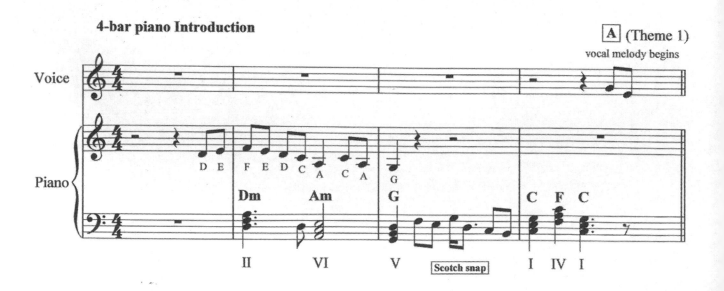

Listen in

Excerpt 11. Complete song harmonised

Now listen to 'Scots Song' in its entirety, complete with **piano accompaniment**, by clicking on the audio icon above (e-book), or accessing the jm-education YouTube video, **'Composing Workshop: excerpts for Scots Song'** (Excerpt 11 at *07.53*) on the jm-education YouTube channel at ***www.youtube/jm-education***. The musical score of the piece is given on pages 80-82, followed by a structure summary on page 83.

Note 1: On the music score, **V7** is the abbreviation used to describe the **dominant seventh chord**, **G7** (containing the four notes **G** (root), **B** (3rd), **D** (5th), **F** (7th)).

Note 2: **V7d** indicates the **dominant seventh chord** (**G7**) in its *third inversion*, where the note **F** (the **interval** a **7th** above **G**), is used as the *lowest* **bass** note.

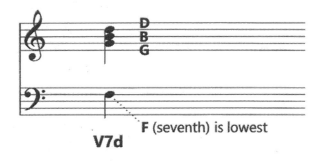

F (seventh) is lowest

V7d

 Activity!

After listening to 'Scots Song' and carefully studying the score, you may want to write a **piano accompaniment** for your own song, including an *Introduction*. Use my **piano accompaniment** part as a guide to aspects such as **style**, **chord** inversions, **contrary motion**, **variation** techniques and so on, and to give yourself some ideas which you may want to develop even further. Just remember not to make the **accompaniment** so busy that it begins to overshadow your **melody**.

An effective method is to **harmonise** the **melody** first of all using just a single **chord** in each bar, then experiment with various **rhythms**, **arpeggios**, **chord** inversions, **passing notes** and so on, listening to what sounds good as you gradually develop the **accompaniment** part a little at a time.

Scots Song

Joe McGowan

Piano accompaniment texture: right hand plays **triads**; left hand plays single note **bass** line which establishes the position of the chord

'Scots Song' Structure Summary

Introduction Bars 1 - 4	A	(Theme 1) Ionian mode - 'major' sound. End of bar 4 - bar 12
One 4-bar phrase based on a **descending melody** containing **dotted crotchet rhythms** and a Scotch snap	Two 4-bar phrases. First phrase introduces the central **rhythms** and mood of the piece, ending with an **imperfect cadence** (bar 8). Second phrase (end of bar 8 - bar 12) **repeats** much of the material of the first phrase with some **variation** added, and ends with a **perfect cadence** (bar 12).	

B (Theme 2) Contrast: '**minor**' sound. End of bar 12 - bar 16.

One 4-bar phrase. Phrase begins at a higher **pitch** and with a **minor** sound created by the chords of **A minor** and **D minor**, ending with an **imperfect cadence** (bar 16).

A1 (Theme 1, first varied repeat) Ionian mode - '**major**' sound. Bar 17 - bar 21.

One 4-bar phrase. Phrase **repeats** material from Theme 1 with some **variation**, including a reversal of the notes in the opening **anacrusis**, and an extension in the length of the **perfect cadence** at the end of the phrase (bars 20 - 21).

C (Theme 3) Contrast: Aeolian mode - '**minor**' sound. Bar 22 - bar 29.

Two 4-bar phrases. First phrase establishes contrasting **minor** sound through the use of the Aeolian mode and the **chords** of **A minor** and **E minor** (**tonic** and **dominant** chords (**I** and **V**) in the Aeolian mode). Second phrase introduces a new **semiquaver rhythm** in bars 27 and 29, ending with an **imperfect cadence** at bar 29.

A2 (Theme 1, second varied repeat) Ionian mode - '**major**' sound. End of bar 29 - bar 38.

Two 4-bar phrases, both of which **repeat** much of the material of Theme 1 with some **variation**, including the addition of an extra bar in **2/4 time** (bar 38) to extend the duration of the **perfect cadence** at the end of the second phrase.

D (Piano instrumental) Aeolian mode - '**minor**' sound. Bar 39 - bar 46.

Two 4-bar phrases. The instrumental section consists of a **repeat** of Theme 3, where the **piano** plays both **melody** and **accompaniment**.

A3 Coda (3rd varied repeat of Theme 1) Ionian mode - '**major**' sound. End of bar 46 - bar 63.

Two phrases of irregular length. The **Coda** is based on a **varied repeat** of Theme 1, where the **metre** is changed to **3/4 time** and **augmentation** used on some of the notes, creating the feeling that the music is slowing down for a more expressive conclusion.

Adding Lyrics

At the start of this workshop I mentioned that I would not be writing lyrics to 'Scots Song' but that you could do so for your own song (*and* mine, if you fancy a little extra practice).

Your lyrics will have to fit with the *mood* and *style* of the song as well as its **rhythms** and phrase structure, and you should consider the use of both **melismatic** and **syllabic** vocal writing. Just try to let the atmosphere of the **melody** conjure up ideas and images in your mind which you can convert into words.

If at a later stage you decide to compose another song or ballad based on an existing text such as a poem (or perhaps lyrics you have written yourself), you can still, of course, follow the various composing steps used in this workshop, ensuring that your **themes** (or **verses** and **choruses**) fit the **rhythm** of your chosen words.

Extension Ideas

Arranging 'Scots Song' **for a larger instrumental group**

With the music and lyrics of your song written, you could go on to expand the piece by adding more instruments, perhaps arranging it for a **folk group** or even a small **choir** (with or without the **piano accompaniment**).

Developing 'Scots Song' **using a Digital Audio Workstation (DAW)**

Alternatively, you might choose to arrange your song using a computer and a Digital Audio Workstation (DAW) - also known as a MIDI sequencer - which is how I went on to arrange 'Scots Song'. Using the DAW (or sequencer) I kept the original **piano accompaniment** in the mix but applied several additional instrument sounds (or sound patches) to play the **melody** and **chords**, then added **arpeggios** (derived from the **accompaniment chords**) and a new **bass** part. I also composed a **drum** track which gave extra depth to the music.

For guidelines on electronic music techniques see these resources on the jm-education website:

- How to Pass National 5 Music, Supplementary Material. Chapter 4, Composing and Arranging, *'Electronic Music Workshop: Composing a Dance Track Using a MIDI Sequencer'*

- National 5, Higher and GCSE Music Resources, *Music Technology (instructional videos)*

The chart (or track sheet) on the following page shows details of each track in my DAW arrangement of 'Scots Song'. Note the instrument sounds used for the **melody**, **chord**, **arpeggio** and **bass** parts, and how some of these only play at certain sections in the arrangement; this kind of variety helps to create an interesting sound mix. Another very important aspect of the mix is the *volume level* of each sound; without these different volumes the piece would not be balanced since certain sounds which are naturally louder or have a more prominent **timbre** would overwhelm the others.

TRACK	SOUND PATCH (instrument)	VOLUME (Max = 127)	MUSIC PLAYED
1	Ocarina	90	**Melody** (except at *Instrumental* section)
2	Whistle	80	**Melody** (played two octaves higher than original pitch)
3	Choir Pad	80	**Melody**
4	Piccolo	65	**Melody** (at *Instrumental* section only)
5	Oboe	28	**Melody** (at *Instrumental* section only)
6	Accordion	60	**Melody** at *Coda* section and *arpeggios* in bars 22-30
7	Acoustic grand piano	100	Original **piano accompaniment**
8	Synth strings	40	**Sustained chords** (based on *piano accompaniment*)
9	Hammond organ	40	**Sustained chords** in bars 13-19 and bars 48-65
10	Choir Aahs	45	**Sustained chords** in bars 13-31 and bars 39-65
11	Orchestral harp	50	**Arpeggios** (at *Instrumental* section only) based on *piano accompaniment*)
12	Tubular bells	80	**Single notes** mainly on the first beat of each bar in the *Coda* section
13	Electric bass guitar	65	**Bass part** derived from chords used in the *piano accompaniment*
14	Drums	70	**Basic steady beat** with some links/drum fills

 **Listen in**

Excerpt 12. DAW arrangement

You can hear my full arrangement of '*Scots Song*', produced entirely using the Digital Audio Workstation, by clicking on the audio icon above (e-book), or accessing the jm-education YouTube video, **'Composing Workshop: excerpts for Scots Song'** (Excerpt 12 at *10.55*) on the jm-education YouTube channel at *www.youtube/jm-education*. As an extra guide, the music of the first eight bars of this arrangement is shown below.

The composing review

Of the 30 marks available for the composing assignment, 10 of those are awarded for the composing review (recommended length 200-350 words). The SQA state that, in the composing review, you must:

- Outline the main decisions you have made
- Describe the ways in which you have explored and developed your musical ideas
- Discuss the strengths of the composition and/or areas which may be improved

Below is a sample composing review for 'Scots Song.'

Scots Song composing review

I am interested in traditional Scottish music and wanted to create an original composition in the style of a Scottish ballad. The piece has a lyrical melody line, accompanied by piano, and could be performed as an instrumental duet for piano and another instrument, such as violin, but there is also the option for lyrics to be added.

The piece is broadly structured in rondo form, but within that framework I have added several aspects of variation, including alterations made to each repeat of the 'A' section, and a Coda featuring augmentation and a time signature change from 4/4 to 3/4.

Before starting the composition, I listed the central elements that would create a 'Scottish' sound, including Scotch snaps, dotted rhythms, instruments used in folk music (incorporated in my DAW arrangement), and the use of modes.

Next, I outlined a structure diagram of the main sections and what each of these may feature, including a piano introduction and coda flanking the main A,B,A,C,A,D rondo structure.

I began improvising on piano with the Ionian mode and the C pentatonic major scale and came up with a 4-bar phrase which would form a 'question' phrase for which I then composed a 4-bar answer phrase. This became the basis of the recurring 'A' theme in my song, which I would vary slightly on each subsequent repeat.

For contrast in Sections B and C I focused on both the Aeolian mode and the minor chords in the Ionian mode, whilst section D is a piano instrumental based on the music of section C. Finally, I wrote the Coda in 3/4 time for variation (and to emphasise the conclusion), followed by a 4-bar piano introduction influenced by some of the melodic ideas used throughout the piece.

I would say the strength of this piece is that it has a solid structure and uses musical concepts in a carefully-considered and coherent way. Perhaps one area that could be improved is the left hand (chord) part for the piano which at times seems a bit repetitive and could possibly benefit from having slightly more rhythmic variety.

Chapter 5 Performing

Course requirements

In Higher Music you are required to perform on **two** different musical instruments (one of which can be **voice**). Your performance can involve **solo** playing and/or playing as part of a **group** of other musicians.

For example, you might choose from one of these options:

- Perform on **two** musical instruments
- Perform on **one** musical instrument **and** voice
- Perform on **one** solo musical instrument **and** a different instrument **as part of a group**
- Perform on **solo voice and** an instrument **as part of a group**

Instrument choice

You can choose from **two** of the instruments listed in the table below. **Note**: some instrument combinations are not permitted (for example, those from the same family - such as acoustic guitar and electric guitar). For the list of approved instrument combinations refer to *Higher Music Course Specification - Approved instruments and combinations of instruments* on the SQA website.

Accordion (free bass or Stradella	**Organ (pipe)**
Bagpipes (Scottish)	**Piano**
Baritone and Euphonium	**Pipe band drumming**
Bassoon	**Recorder (descant)**
Bass guitar	**Recorder (treble)**
Cello	**Saxophone (alto and baritone)**
Clarinet	**Saxophone (soprano and tenor)**
Clarsach	**Scots fiddle**
Cornet (E flat)	**Snare drum**
Double bass	**Timpani**
Drum kit	**Tin whistle**
Flute	**Trombone (tenor)**
Guitar (classical)	**Trumpet (B flat cornet and flugel)**
Guitar (acoustic and electric)	**Tuba**
Harp	**Tuned percussion**
Horn in F	**Ukelele**
Horn (tenor)	**Viola**
Keyboard (electronic)	**Violin**
Oboe	**Voice**

Assessment

During your Higher Music course, and with the guidance of your music teacher and/or music instrumental tutor, you will work towards preparing a performance programme lasting a **minimum** of **12 minutes** and **maximum** of **13 minutes**. The performance can be **solo** and/or **in a group setting** and the performance time on either of the two selected instruments, or instrument and voice, must be a **minimum of 4 minutes** within the overall **12-13 minute** programme.

Take Note

For more detailed information on the assessment procedure see:
'The Performance' page 120

Candidates should perform a minimum of **two** contrasting pieces of music on each of the two selected instruments, or instrument and voice. These should be of an appropriate standard/level of difficulty, which is **grade 4** or above (see page ix for websites where you can obtain information on suitable grade 4 level pieces for your instrument or voice).

The marking procedure is:

- **Performance instrument 1 (marked by a visiting assessor) 30 marks**
- **Performance instrument 2 (marked by a visiting assessor) 30 marks**

The **60 marks** available represent a scaled mark of **50% of the total overall mark** for your Higher Music course. Each piece of music in the programme will be given a mark out of 10, but as the number of pieces in the programme is variable within the prescribed time restrictions, scaling will be used to determine the final mark.

Great advice...
Top Tip

No special talent required

You do not need to have a natural gift or special talent for playing an instrument in order to excel as a musician - those things just give a player a bit of a head start. Talent means little if two far more important qualities are not present:

1. The **desire** to play the instrument (or sing)

2. The **willingness** to **practise** regularly

Without these, even the most naturally talented players will not succeed.

Imagine life with no music..!

Without musicians learning to play and perform on musical instruments (including the human voice) and use computer Digital Audio Workstations (DAWs) there simply wouldn't be any music. It's why all the other stuff (musical concepts, composing, literacy/theory) exists at all. Musical performance, therefore, is really the driving force behind all musical study.

Of course you don't have to play a musical instrument or sing to enjoy or study music, but the ability to perform in a way that makes people (especially you) feel something - uplifted, motivated, relaxed, sad, moved - is surely one of the most rewarding things a human being can do. It must be, otherwise we wouldn't have been doing it for thousands of years!

If it was too easy we couldn't impress anyone

Like anything worthwhile, learning to play an instrument or sing well can at times be challenging, but the rewards will justify the effort involved in confronting and overcoming those challenges. People admire musical talent, and those who don't play an instrument are often amazed by the skill of those who can - including their ability to read all the notes, signs and symbols of music notation.

So, learning to play a musical instrument (or sing) is definitely a worthy activity - and it needn't be difficult if you listen to the advice offered by experienced people such as music teachers and performing musicians (and jm-education!) who want to help make your journey as straightforward and enjoyable as possible.

Take some free professional advice (from the older dudes...)

Your music teacher and/or instrumental tutor will be your main guide for the performing component of the course, but this chapter gives you loads of extra tips and guidance which, hopefully, will prove useful not only for the duration of Higher Music, but throughout your life should you continue to perform music.

As a student of Higher Music it is likely that you have previously studied National 5 Music and been introduced to some practice and performance techniques (several of which are outlined in the book, *How to Pass National 5 Music*). If so, then the following pages will not only provide a reminder of these, but also an opportunity to further develop your performing skills since, in this book, we go into more detail with practice strategies and performance preparation.

From sourcing reliable advice and resources to adopting good practice techniques and preparing for live performances, let us now pass on some of the experience we have accumulated over many years in the music business!

Choosing your music

Standard of music to be performed

Each piece of music chosen for performance must be of an appropriate level for Higher Music. Your class teacher or instrumental tutor will help you with this selection, but as a guide all music should be at least **grade 4** level as outlined in the syllabuses of the various music schools. See the *'Essential online resources'* table on page ix for the websites of the schools where individual syllabuses for your chosen instrument(s) can usually be downloaded for free.

Choose carefully

As well as choosing music of an appropriate level, it is essential that you select pieces you really like and will enjoy playing. Don't choose music simply because it is of the right standard, or because someone else you know likes or recommends it; you could quickly become bored practising such music and there may be little sense of achievement when you can finally play it. Learning something you really *want* to be able to play will provide the motivation to practise it.

Sources of help and professional advice

In addition to your class teacher, there are several other sources that could prove very helpful.

A music tutor

You may be fortunate enough to have a one-to-one weekly lesson with an instructor such as a guitar or piano teacher, voice coach etc. - either at school or on a private basis - who specialises in your chosen instrument(s). Such an experienced tutor will help you with aspects of technique, repertoire and performing that will enable you to progress efficiently and much quicker than might otherwise be the case. Their job is to act as a friendly guide, providing solutions for any difficulties you encounter along the way and steering you clear of potential pitfalls as you advance through progressively higher levels.

Online resources

A fantastic thing about the Internet is the sheer volume of musical resources available - including live and recorded lessons, sheet music and tabs, backing tracks and chords/lyrics for thousands of songs. It's also possible to hear others playing the music you intend to learn for your performing exam (professionals and amateurs alike), and this can be a great source of reference and learning.

Online tuition

Live online lessons from tutors (via Skype, Facetime, Google hangouts etc.) are growing in popularity and can be a convenient way to get some helpful extra tuition - but be careful to check the reputation and qualifications of any tutor offering this service. A professional tutor will be pleased to provide information about their qualifications and experience, so don't be afraid to ask before paying for any lessons.

Even if you don't receive any form of live music tuition, on various websites you can still access free online instructional/tutorial videos and resource material relating to the instrument(s) you play. However, as with online tuition, you must be careful that any resource you access comes from a reliable source - ideally prepared by an accredited professional - to ensure that you are getting good, accurate advice. Your class teacher may be able to guide you with this.

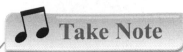

Take Note

Check online resources

There are some great musical resources online, but a lot of poor and unreliable material is also posted by inexperienced people. It is therefore very important to ensure that any information you obtain has come from a trustworthy source, so always check the reputation of unfamiliar websites, look for helpful user comments, or ask your music teacher/instructor for advice. Online music tuition and professional advice - from single lessons and exam coaching to regular mentoring - is available from **www.yourmusicmentor.com** which is affiliated with jm-education.

Backing tracks

(See Part 3, *Improvisation*, pages 111-114 for advice on using backing tracks)

Music backing tracks are a tremendously useful free online resource that can help develop your improvising, singing and group performing skills - and they're also great fun to use! There are thousands of tracks available in every **style**, **key** and **tempo** variation on a number of sites (YouTube probably being the most common), so you can select those which suit your playing ability and musical preferences.

Song lyrics with accompanying chords/tabs

(See pages 106-111 for advice on using this resource and page 114 for a list of useful websites)

Several websites specialise in providing thousands of songs in lyric-and-chord format (song lyrics with **accompaniment chords** shown above the words), or lyric-and-tab format (a system that uses numbers to indicate where each note of a song **melody** can be found on a **guitar** fret board).

On a few sites you can also play along with a song video - where you follow the **chords** while they scroll on screen as the music progresses - and it's even possible to slow down the music to make it easier to practise. This is like having your own private band ready to play live whenever you want!

Tutor books

Most practical music tutor books (those devoted to teaching a musical instrument) are actually intended for use with teachers and their students rather than just the student working alone. However, some do claim that they can show you how to 'teach yourself' using their method, usually with linked online resources such as videos or interactive material to make the learning process more effective, personal and enjoyable.

These books can be useful, particularly for anyone who just wants to try out a new instrument, or who intends to attain only a basic level of ability, but the student must be very careful to work through the steps methodically and pay careful attention to the instructions given as there will be no tutor on hand to spot and correct errors.

However, no book can fully interact with a student or answer every question that may arise, so if you are serious about learning to play or perform well then there is little substitute for having an experienced tutor to guide you through the process.

Suggestions for effective practice

'I love music and the prospect of being able to play an instrument and sing well, if only the practice wasn't so tedious and I could progress quicker. There are even parts of some pieces of music that are so tricky I wonder if I'll ever be able to play them fluently...'

If that sounds familiar, don't worry; it's a common response that says more about how a student is practising than their musical ability. Learning to play/sing and perform well begins with learning how to practise well, and that usually means re-evaluating what practice *is*, and how to get the most out of it, and yourself, as a developing musician.

We all know that the only way to improve on a musical instrument (including voice) is to practise regularly, but that shouldn't involve forcing ourselves to go into a room for a set period of time each day, routinely playing through music and scales in the belief that that is the only way to succeed. This unfortunately common approach can quickly become dull, reducing the rate of progress when there are actually far more effective and enjoyable strategies you can use.

A common misconception about music practice

Most people assume that longer practice sessions result in better playing, but if you're only playing the same things over and over then you could be wasting a lot of time simply repeating the same mistakes. Repetition alone will not 'fix' difficult parts or performance weaknesses which have to be targeted in a more specific way. This is often the reason why students feel they are not progressing well, or have even reached a complete standstill. Improving your playing ability involves knowing how to target the areas that need to be improved.

Great advice... **Top Tip**

Start with the right attitude: it's not just about *how often* you practise but *HOW* you practise

Twenty minutes of focused practice that targets the weaker areas of your playing is worth an hour or more spent going through the routine of just playing a selection of pieces several times. Knowing how to get the most out of every minute you spend practising will accelerate your learning and help you avoid some of the common errors that can slow down or even halt your progress.

Want to learn quicker and play better?
Get a good practice strategy!

Practice equation

Less time required to learn new music = more enjoyable practice + increased sense of achievement + motivation

= Good practice strategy

I prefer to use the term practice *strategy* rather than practice *routine* for two reasons:

1. Although regular practice is vital for progress, your practice sessions don't have to follow a routine pattern each time. You can vary what you do and 'mix things up' a little.

2. The approaches outlined in the following pages may seem more like a clever strategy than practice techniques once you start to see the positive results.

In order to improve steadily most students need to practise better, not more, and this starts inside the head.

Be friends with your brain!

Every physical movement or sound you make begins as a command sent from your brain to the body parts or muscles required to perform the desired action. Lungs, mouth, diaphragm, vocal cords and tongue are used when we sing or play a wind instrument. The drums demand coordinated use of arms, hands and one foot (for the bass drum pedal). Stringed instruments and piano need more precise articulation of the fingers.

It's a fascinating neurological process, but the most important thing to remember is that it all starts in the *brain*. It stands to reason, therefore, that if you 'input' precisely the information outlined on the printed music, tab, chord/lyric sheet or whatever, your brain will then send accurate signals to their destination and you'll play/sing the music correctly.

Compare that with how we sometimes just open a sheet of music and attempt to play through it without having first taken any time to understand everything that's printed on the page. This is sight reading, and it's the slowest way to learn because it involves only skimming through the music rather than really learning it as we stumble through numerous inaccuracies and mistakes - as opposed to stopping to consider *why* we're making those mistakes.

Many students practise this way believing that repetition alone will eventually smooth out the inaccuracies, but, apart from being a very time-consuming process, this approach also increases the likelihood that some errors with notes or **rhythm** will go unnoticed, and difficult passages remain difficult because the player hasn't explored ways to make them easier. Then, when the pressure is on during a live performance, that player will dread having to play these parts and just trust to luck that they work out alright on the day. This is definitely NOT a good approach!

Getting it right from the very start will avoid this scenario and enable you to prevent or fix mistakes, thereby saving you lots of precious time that can be spent making constant progress.

There are several useful approaches for learning and practising music, whether using standard notation, tabs, chord & lyric sheets, or just your ear, so let's take a look at some of these.

Take Note

If the brain isn't given all the correct information it can't send the correct signals, and repetition alone will not fix that - you'll just keep repeating the same mistakes.

Part 1: Reading standard music notation - easy as 1,2,3...4

1. Stop and look

Having established that good practising starts with supplying the brain with the correct information, and that learning to play a new piece of music should NOT be treated as a sight reading exercise, the first thing to do is have a good *look* at the music, noting things such as:

- **the basic structure**
- **beats in the bar**
- **key signature**
- **note values**
- **repeated bars**
- **repeated sections**
- **rhythm patterns**
- **dynamics**

2. Turn the piece into a jigsaw...

Like a jigsaw, a piece of music is made up of lots of different component parts - notes, bars, sections etc. - that make up the whole. If we regard each bar of music as a separate piece of the jigsaw, this can help with the learning process. Here's how...

Unless the piece is **through-composed** it will have elements such as repeated **bars**, **rhythms** or **sections** - patterns - that give it structure. Most songs, for example, have a very clear structure of repeated vocal **phrases**, **verses** and **choruses**. These elements can be indicated on the page (or sheet music) in the following way:

1. Using a pencil, start mapping out the *obvious* main sections of the music you see by enclosing brackets around these and labelling them as section *A, B, C,* etc. Main sections often begin or end where **repeat signs**/bars or a **Da Capo** instruction occur, or where you can see that several bars of music are repeating material used previously. From this the main structure of the piece (i.e. **binary**, **ternary**, **rondo**, **verse-chorus-verse**) should become clear.

2. Next, look carefully at the music within these main sections and note all repetitions of single bars or phrases in the same way, perhaps indicating these with numbers rather than letters this time so they don't become confused with the sections.

3. Note other smaller details now such as recurring **rhythms** and note patterns, as well as any technically challenging bars or phrases that will require careful attention.

3. Practise the individual 'pieces' of the jigsaw separately

With all the large and small components now clearly indicated, the whole piece should now look a lot more straightforward, and certainly things like patterns and repetition will be far more obvious. Being able to see clearly just how many original bars there are compared to those which are simply repeated is very useful when practising, since you need only work on the original bars to 'fast track' through the learning process. Then it's just a matter of linking up all the bars, including the repeated ones, to put the entire piece of music together.

Great advice... **Top Tip**

Always start... anywhere you like

Just as a jigsaw is built in little sections in no predetermined order, a piece of music can be learned in the same way. You don't have to start at the beginning of the piece and work through the bars consecutively; you can begin anywhere you like - perhaps with the easiest parts or the most difficult - or work in random sections. You might even start at the end and work backwards towards the beginning!

Sometimes it's good to get off to a nice slow start...

- **Start slowly**. If you don't take things slowly at the start when practising a new piece you could easily overlook details in the music or fail to notice errors until much later, or until these are pointed out to you. When this happens it can be difficult to 'unlearn' the habit of playing with the inaccuracies, not to mention the significant waste of time that could have been avoided.

- **Practise in small sections**. You might focus on a few bars - or even just one - at a time, not moving on until you get them right. It often helps to see a complete piece of music as a composite of lots of 'mini pieces' that make up the whole, and treat each of these small sections with equal respect. In more challenging music you can even divide individual bars into smaller parts.

- **Separate the notes and rhythm**. Sometimes reading both the musical notes and the **rhythm** at the same time can prove challenging. This could be because the music is 'busy' with lots of notes, or because the **rhythm** is complex - perhaps both. When this is the case it makes sense to separate notes and **rhythm** and practise them individually. Try this:

Step 1. Take time to ensure you are reading all the notes in the bar/passage correctly and, if appropriate, work out the fingering that will best enable you to play them as fluently as possible. Taking a little time to work out a good, articulate fingering will make difficult passages much easier to play.

Step 2. Work out the **rhythm** and clap or tap it several times, slowly, until you are confident you've got it right and it starts to become automatic. You may find it helpful to use a metronome for this and count the **rhythm** out loud; for example: '*1 and 2 e-and-a 3, 4 and-a.*'

After undertaking the above two steps you should then find it much easier to combine both notes and **rhythm** in any bar or passage of music.

- **Isolate the more challenging parts and practise them separately**. During your analysis of the piece, you will probably have identified some bars or passages that are more demanding than others. These should be practised carefully on their own.

Isolating the tricky parts and working on them separately is an effective way to master them more quickly - and indeed, the whole piece. If you don't target the challenges in this way, or believe they will just 'sort themselves out in time', they are likely to remain weak areas in the music that threaten to trip you up when you are playing under performance pressure. So it's best to deal with them early on.

Take Note

When slow is quicker

Spending some time working on just one or two bars of music might sound painfully slow and boring, but it could save you months trying to get a whole piece to sound right when in fact only a few bars need careful attention.

Learning new or demanding music by playing it slowly allows you to absorb all the elements correctly, whereas rushing through it only results in misread notes and wrongly played **rhythms** that will have to be corrected later. By all means have a quick play through of the piece to get the feel of it, but be aware this is not focused learning, it's sight reading, and that is a different activity. So get things right from the start and you won't waste time.

Remember: Ten minutes spent working carefully on the difficult parts can fix problems that ten weeks spent skimming over them won't. So, practising slowly is actually the quickest and most efficient way to learn!

Take Note

Repetition alone isn't enough

Simply playing a difficult part over and over won't always make it easier; you might just keep playing it wrong lots of times. This will only decrease your confidence and cause you to tense up in anticipation of that part approaching each time you play the piece, thereby increasing the likelihood of making a mistake. You'll have to slow down to discover exactly what's *causing* the problem (playing too fast? Unsure about the notes? Rhythm?), then go about fixing it so that it becomes as straightforward as other parts of the piece.

The importance of good technique

Good vocal or instrumental technique allows you to sing/play better, and in most cases it will also make learning new music easier, since weak technique only creates obstacles that needn't be there. Things like slouching; tension in the arms/body; bad posture; hands or arms in an awkward position and inefficient breath control will produce poor technique and impede your progress, making performing harder and some music beyond your capability.

Working on technique improves articulation, fluency and speed, breathing, bowing, tone, tonguing and phrasing. It takes a little time to develop but the rewards make it well worth the effort, so be patient! Here are the main things to consider:

- **Check you are applying good technique every time you practise.** Are you relaxed? Is there too much tension in your arms or body? Are you sitting and holding the instrument or sticks/beaters correctly? Are you controlling your breathing well? Are you maintaining good posture and hand position? Make sure you know the basics of good technique for your chosen instrument(s) and *always* observe them.

- **Choose your fingers carefully!** For string and keyboard players, the particular finger sequence used to play a bar or passage of music is of greater importance than many inexperienced players realise. Thinking carefully about which fingers are used to play successive notes can make stretches, chords and fast or demanding passages far more manageable and fluent, as well as reduce tension in the hands and arms. Sometimes the suggested fingering printed on the music may not be the best option for every player, so always be prepared to consider alternative fingerings which might be more effective for you. This is especially important if you don't have a teacher or instructor to advise you on this very important aspect of instrumental technique.

You only have two hands - use them well!

When working out a good fingering for the music in a bar you MUST also take into account the previous bar and the one that follows, since each bar must flow into the other with no awkward finger movements or unnecessary position changes. This will ensure that you are playing entire phrases as articulately as possible.

Carefully considered fingering will simplify bars and phrases and help them to flow, ultimately making an entire piece easier, whereas inefficient fingering can make everything much harder to accomplish. **That's how important it is to choose your fingers carefully!**

Technique is the engine, but you are the driver

All the stuff you learn about technique - how to hold a musical instrument properly, articulate your fingers, project your voice etc. - deals with the essential *mechanics* that will make it *physically* easier for you to play more effectively, but remember that *musicianship* (the way you express or 'feel' the music) is an ability that's already present inside you, just waiting to be accessed. Technique assists musical performance, but you make the music.

Don't pull a music muscle; warm up first!

Don't begin a practice session with technically demanding music; always warm up your voice/muscles/fingers first with easier material (such as scales or perhaps something from your repertoire) before moving on to more challenging music. Warming up improves your physical/vocal flexibility and can prevent discomfort and even possible minor injury - just as it does in sporting activity!

4. Putting it all together

- **Play in sections**. Once you have the basic literacy elements of notes and **rhythm** worked out, along with any particularly challenging areas of the piece, you can then start playing the various sections of the music. Depending on how demanding the piece, this could involve a main section, single lines, or smaller passages of just a few bars. Play each of these parts at least five times in succession and at a comfortable **tempo** that allows you to remain relaxed, without making errors.

- **Steady play through**. When each section is fluent, it's time to put them all together to complete the 'jigsaw' and play the piece all the way through.

- **Slowly at first, gradually building up the speed**. Attempting to play a new piece of music at the suggested **tempo** (especially if it is fast) before you have first become completely familiar with its various elements will result in performance errors that make you tense up - which only triggers even more mistakes. For the first few performances of the whole piece you must play slowly enough to remain relaxed in the knowledge that you will be able to play whatever is coming up next in the music. Playing slowly also enables you to *listen* to how well you are performing and interpreting the piece. You can then increase the speed gradually as your confidence grows, until the desired **tempo** is reached. If you start making mistakes at any time, just reduce the speed a little and gradually build it up again.

- **Don't keep going back to the start**. If you keep making a mistake at a particular point in the music then you obviously have to focus more on that area. Don't go back to the very beginning each time and start over. What is the point of playing the first ten bars again if bar eleven is causing you a problem? Focus only on the tricky part.

- *Why do I always make a mess of the fast bits..?* The inability to play fast passages of music usually has nothing to do with the fact that the fingers, arms or voice aren't physically capable, but rather that the technique needs improving. The player may also be expecting his/her brain to keep up with the music without fully understanding what is required technically - as though their brain should somehow just 'magically' know what to do! So, remember:

1. Take time to 'upload' the correct information from the printed music to your brain
2. Make sure your playing technique is as good as it can be
3. Break up fast or technically demanding passages into smaller sections and practise these slowly before piecing everything back together
4. Gradually increase the speed, making sure all notes and **rhythms** remain clear and accurate and you are playing in a regular beat.

For faster progress, apply basic logic, not speed!

If you can't play a piece all the way through slowly without making mistakes, why would you expect to be able to play it faster without errors? Learn to play the music first at a **tempo** where you feel relaxed and in control, then gradually increase the speed and you'll be surprised at how much quicker you achieve the desired result.

Feeling vs Speed

Playing fast when you are not quite ready will put you under unnecessary pressure and demand more concentration for technical issues rather than expression and phrasing. The result can be correct notes but music without feeling. Music played at a slow or moderate **tempo** with character and emotion is better than a fast performance that sounds like a machine is playing!

- **Details**. Once you are happy that you can play through a piece without making persistent mistakes caused by uncertainty about what's happening in any part of the music - or because you're playing too fast - you can then apply whatever expressive musical features are indicated, such as **dynamics**, **staccato**, **accents**, **crescendos** etc. These things suggest how to convey the feeling or mood intended by the composer, so pay close attention to them.

- **Assess your playing**. Regularly ask yourself: *'How might I improve my performance or express the character or emotion of the music better?'* Don't try to fool yourself; you will know when something's not quite right with the piece or your playing. When this happens don't just skim over the weak area in the hope that you'll get it right next time. Remember, if something's not right it will only be fixed if *you* isolate and remedy the problem. Otherwise, you'll only end up dreading the difficult part and hoping that, by sheer luck, it'll work out okay in the next performance. Tackle the difficulties head on and your music will flow!

- **Listen**. Always listen carefully as you play to make sure you are making a good sound and bringing out the character or emotion of the music as well as you can. If it moves you it will probably move your audience, too.

The advantage of memorising music

Committing a whole piece of music to memory - or even just the trickier parts - will allow you to focus more on the performance as you won't have to keep referring to pages of music notation. Becoming familiar with a piece in this way is a great advantage when the pressure is on.

Memorising music doesn't always just 'happen' by playing something over and over, so you'll have to actively work on committing a piece to memory. This can be done by focusing on bars one at a time until whole lines then sections are memorised, and finally the entire piece.

The reason why simply reading/playing through a whole piece of music many times doesn't always result in that piece being stored in the memory is because the brain is relying on *sight* each time and therefore doesn't *need* to access memory. You can actively kick start the memorisation process by reducing the brain's reliance on the sense of sight and making it more dependent on things like internal visualisation (the mind's eye), touch and muscle memory (the instinctive recollection of the physical 'feel' of rhythmic patterns, note passages, chord sequences etc).

2-Step memorisation technique

(See also Easy techniques for memorising chord progressions in songs, page 108)

1. Try reading/playing a bar of music then look away from the notation and see if you can repeat it from memory. It may be you remember some bits but not others. If this happens have another look, focusing on the part you couldn't recall, and try again. As soon as you can confidently play the bar from memory, move to the next one and repeat the process. When you have memorised the second bar join it to the first and play both bars from memory a few times.

2. Continue this process with each successive bar, adding one new bar each time until you have a whole line or section committed to memory. Next, after taking a short break of between fifteen and thirty minutes, see if you can play the memorised passage again. If you have forgotten anything or aren't absolutely sure about a particular part, look back at the music to refresh your memory then try the whole section again.

Activating these internal visualisation and muscle memory processes - or teaching yourself to instinctively feel the patterns - is what allows professional musicians (whether they read music or not) to commit entire pieces to memory. Rock and pop musicians, for example, use similar processes all the time (usually without referring to music notation) to prepare an entire gig of music/songs.

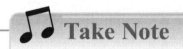

Take Note

Always double check

It is important to return to the printed music now and again just to make sure you haven't remembered anything incorrectly!

After a few weeks you will notice that you are developing new memorisation skills; building up pictures of the music in your mind's eye and allowing muscle memory to guide you instinctively through the various patterns, phrases and physical movements in a piece. This can make you feel more deeply involved in everything you play, and generally more confident about performing.

Anyone, no matter what their level, can practise like a professional

Professional musicians know how to practise efficiently, and that includes using many of the techniques described in the last few pages. Making mistakes is part of learning new music but, as we have seen, many can be avoided if you have an effective practice strategy in place.

This strategy should become a good habit that prevents other bad habits from developing - such as poor technique - which will slow down your progress. You may not be a professional musician, but you can certainly practise like one!

Top Tip

'I've been playing this piece for months and can't seem to get it right - especially this one bit in the middle...'

Does that sound familiar? Have you ever said or thought something like this about a piece of music you've been learning? If the answer is *yes*, then ask yourself the following questions: Have I ever sat down and examined the difficult bit(s) to see whether a more effective fingering could be used? Have I worked on the notes and **rhythm** separately? Have I played the part several times at a slow, controlled speed that allows me to focus on both **rhythm** and note accuracy? Have I treated the problem area with enough respect, really got to 'know' it, as though it's a mini piece of music in its own right?

Take Note

Recipe for success: add 2 parts lesson to 8 parts practice...

It is often said that practical music lessons equate to about 20 percent of what is required to play well, with practice making up the remaining 80 percent. Based on that calculation, if you have a 30 minute weekly lesson, around three hours should be devoted to practising every week. Broken down, that is 30 minutes practice a day for 6 days each week.

Take Note

'Can't' is just a temporary condition

If you can't do something it usually just means you can't do it *yet* because you haven't devoted enough time to learning. It certainly doesn't mean you can't do it and will *never* be able to. Patience and determination are more important than special talents, so never allow excuses or a negative attitude to get in the way of your progress.

Take Note

Music practice cannot be 'crammed'

Playing a musical instrument or singing is a physical activity as much as an intellectual one, meaning that regular practice is important for keeping muscles or vocal cords warmed up and supple, as well as developing the kind of muscle memory that will allow you to play music instinctively.

So, missing a couple of days of practice and then having a mammoth one and a half hour session on the third day, believing you can 'catch up', could possibly do more harm than good. Your fingers will probably ache, muscles (or voice) could feel stressed and over-used, and everything will seem more demanding. Habitually practising this way could even cause some physical damage such as a strain injury.

 Take Note

Make practice a pleasure, not a pain

Practising a musical instrument isn't (and shouldn't feel like) homework; something that is expected of you because it's part of a curriculum of subjects. You have chosen to study music and learn an instrument presumably because you enjoy music and *want* to play it well. Therefore, if anything, music practice should be an escape from other studies where you can be free to express yourself while learning at the same time.

 Take Note

We practise not only to learn music but also to maintain it

Regular music practice isn't just for learning new pieces but also maintaining the standard of those we can already play; our *repertoire* pieces. It also develops physical dexterity, breath control, muscle memory and a whole load of other things which result in the ability to perform music better and with much less effort. This leads to the kind of instinctive playing that will allow you to enjoy performing a lot more.

Will it help to hear a recording of a piece before starting to learn it?

'It's easier for me to play a piece of music if I know what it should sound like.' This is a comment music students often make because, after all, most of us choose to learn a particular piece of music because we've first heard it and liked it. However, whilst it's essential to be familiar with a piece of music (by ear) if you are using guitar tabs or working out a specific improvisation, the same isn't necessarily true when using music notation. That's because replaying a piece in your head can easily deflect your full attention away from the printed music as you'll be accessing a memory (which might not be completely accurate), and therefore increasing the risk of errors with notes, **rhythm** or beat.

Record yourself

The mind can sometimes play tricks by blocking out such inaccuracies and you will only hear what you *want* to hear, or what you *think* is right. A good way to check that you are playing accurately (apart from having your teacher listen) is to record yourself and listen carefully to the playback. You might be a little surprised at the flaws that went unnoticed because you were trying to *remember* notes and **rhythms** rather than reading and *counting* them properly.

Checking performance accuracy in this way is especially important if you are a soloist since you won't have another player or group member to point out any inaccuracies during practice.

Another thing to watch out for when you have heard a piece of music many times is that you don't just end up copying another player's interpretation of it. Sometimes you may want to do exactly that, of course, but in most cases you could be denying yourself the opportunity to interpret the piece your own way and make it more personally expressive and sincere. These are musical qualities that will be transferred to your audience and improve their experience, so don't be a copy artist, be a good musician!

 **Take Note**

Leave copying other people to parrots!

Your musical skills are tested and developed more when you work on music you've never heard before. That's because you can't be guided or distracted by the memory of a tune playing inside your head while you are reading the music.

Part 2: learning songs/music without music notation

Guitar tab

Guitar tab (short for guitar *tablature*) is a system of notating a piece of music for the instrument using lines (representing the guitar strings) and numbers (indicating the frets). Although tab can be a quick way to learn where to locate the correct notes on the guitar to play a song or piece of music, unlike music notation the musical **rhythm** is seldom displayed, meaning the player needs to know exactly how a piece sounds before the method can be used. Also, it isn't possible to sight read guitar tab as all the information can't be processed quickly enough.

However, tab can be very useful for guitarists or bass guitarists in a band who want to learn **riffs** or **solos** from memory. It's also sometimes used for **ukulele** and **banjo** music.

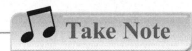 Take Note

First, get into your rhythm

If using guitar tab, care must be taken to completely familiarise yourself with the piece of music you're learning by listening to a recording of it several times to ensure you really know the correct **rhythms**. That's because, normally, only the location of each note (not the **rhythm**) will be given in guitar tab.

Song lyrics with chords

Many music websites provide song lyrics with **accompaniment chords** shown above each word where a **chord change** occurs. The songs on these sites are listed alphabetically and can therefore be accessed quickly for reference or download. Most also have a **key** transposition facility, meaning the **key** can be changed to suit different voice ranges or present **chords** that are easier to play.

Although **guitar**, **ukulele** or **piano accompaniment chords** are often displayed, the lyrics and chords provided on this type of website will be useful to all musicians playing within a group setting, whatever their chosen instrument(s).

At first glance the information on these song sheets can seem like a lot to remember, especially if the song is more than two pages in length. But, as with reading music notation, if you have a careful look you'll most likely see **repetition** or patterns that reveal a straightforward structure - one that will make memorisation much easier.

An easy memorisation method

Unless the song is entirely **through-composed** (very unlikely) there will be two main recurring elements: **verses** and **choruses**. The **chorus** will of course be repetitive, with both its lyrics and **chord** progressions probably remaining the same through the whole song, which means you'll only need to learn one **chord** progression to cover every **chorus** in the song.

The same may well be true for the **chord** progressions of the **verses**, where the lyrics change but the **chords** might not. Other sections of the song may include an intro, a **bridge** or **middle 8**, an outro (or **Coda**) etc., but look at these carefully as they, too, may be a **repeat** or partial **repeat** of a **chord** progression already used in the song's **verses** or **chorus**.

Having examined the song sheet for **repeats** and patterns, you can then note all of your observations on the sheet using a pencil to mark sections as *Intro, Verse 1, Verse 2, Chorus 1, Chorus 2, Link, Bridge, Middle 8, Coda* etc., if these are not already indicated. You will now see patterns and structure even more clearly, and it's not uncommon at this stage to realise that the song only consists of two or three different chord progressions, even though there are lots of chord changes indicated on the page.

Take Note

Always get a second opinion

Occasionally, some inaccurate **chords** can be displayed on a lyric-and-chord sheet, so play through the **chord** sequences to ensure that they sound true to the original music. It's also a good idea to cross-check with other versions of the song, and search on the most reliable websites.

Rely on your ears to discover exactly where the chord changes occur

Although **chord changes** will usually appear in the correct place on the page above the word on which they occur, this can't always be relied upon since glitches in the layout - or the inexperience of the person who has edited and posted the song - can affect the accuracy of what is indicated. Also, a singer may have used **rubato** or their own preferred phrasing in a recording you have heard - as opposed to singing words or syllables precisely on the beat - so, focusing on the singer on a recording to determine where the **chord changes** occur can sometimes be confusing.

If this happens, it's best to focus on the musical **accompaniment**, rather than the singer, to establish the beats on which **chord changes** take place. If there is a clear **keyboard/synthesizer** or **bass guitar** sound in the music, these instruments can be good to listen to in order to hear where the **harmony** is changing. Start by instinctively tapping your foot or clapping your hands in time with the beat of the music, then, focusing on the music rather than the song lyrics, listen for each **chord change** in the musical **accompaniment**, noting how many taps or claps a **chord** lasted for. Many songs have a straightforward structure where a **chord change** occurs every three or four beats (as in **3/4** and **4/4 time**), but some will be less regular, perhaps with two or more **chord changes** in a bar, or sometimes on the up-beats (**syncopation**), for example.

After a while, you should be able to hear the musical phrases and chords fitting into a regular pattern - this will most commonly be a 4-beat or a 3-beat pattern, meaning the **time signature** is either **4/4** or **3/4**.

This requires concentration and a bit of practice, but you'll soon get the hang of it if you really focus on the main *beat* and the musical **accompaniment** rather than the lyrics. An added advantage is that you will be developing a very valuable listening skill - an essential one to have, in fact, if your performing relies more on **chord** playing than reading music notation or tabs. It will also come in handy for improving your general listening skills and the ability to identify musical concepts!

As soon as you have established the beat pattern (or **time signature**) on the song sheet, you can then draw small vertical lines between the **chords** above the lyrics to indicate bar lines. For example:

$\frac{4}{4}$ C |C |G |F |Am |G |F |Em
Looking at you I can see the future, see the future and a time that never ends.

If there are four steady beats between each **chord** then the **time signature** will of course be **4/4**. If you like, you can write this just before the first word of the song, as above. Note: the bars are of an irregular length only because of the changing number of words in each bar, but the beat stays regular.

Easy techniques for memorising chord progressions in songs

Reduce the song to just its chords and patterns

Once you know on which beats the **chord changes** occur, it will be helpful to memorise the **chord** sequence for the whole song - after all, you probably won't want to take the song sheet on stage with you! **Chord** sequences are often the same in each **verse** or every **repeat** of the **chorus**, so, as an example, we'll examine part of the first **verse** of a song.

Verse 1

$\frac{4}{4}$ C |C |G |F |Am |G |F | Em
Looking at you I can see the future, see the future and a time that never ends.
C |C |G |F |Am |G |F | Em
When will that be, how can it be, if we're only ever just good friends?

To begin, write down just the **chord** sequence on a piece of paper:

$\frac{4}{4}$ | C | C | G | F | Am | G | F | Em | C | C | G | F | Am | G | F | Em

The **chord** sequence of the first sentence is repeated in the second, so everything can be reduced further by adding 'x 2 ' after the first sequence rather than writing it out again.

$\frac{4}{4}$ | C | C | G | F | Am | G | F | Em | x 2

Now the whole section of **verse** has been reduced to just half a line (8 chords) of essential information. **Repetition** or pattern in **chord** sequences often becomes more obvious when the lyrics are removed, thereby simplifying the task of learning and memorising an **accompaniment**. And we can even make that a little easier to remember, too...

Using mnemonics to remember chord progressions

Which do you think would be easier to remember, the **chord** progression **C, C, G, F, Am, G, F, Em, C, C, G, F, Am, G, F, Em,** or the phrase, *Can Cool Giraffes Fly And Gather Five Eggs twice?* Let's find out. Look at the **chord** progression for twenty seconds then close your eyes and see if you can say it aloud from memory, then do the same with the phrase. Which was easier to remember?

It's likely that the words were easier to recall, partly because it's shorter, but mainly because a bizarre little phrase is bound to be more memorable than a plain **chord** progression. The phrase was of course constructed using the successive letters of the first eight **chords** in the progression as the first letters of words I chose randomly - *Can Cool Giraffes Fly And Gather Five Eggs* - with the word *'twice'* added at the end to indicate that the eight **chords** are repeated. *Can Cool Giraffes Fly And Gather Five Eggs twice?*

This is a mnemonic, and these can prove highly effective for memory-jogging when large amounts of plain or hard-to-recall information has to be learnt - especially if the phrase is quirky or bizarre. In fact, the weirder the better!

 Take Note

Don't make a major issue out of something minor

The **chord progression** used in the above example contains an **Am chord**, which could have been noted in the mnemonic by adding an extra word beginning with the letter 'M'. For example, *Can Cool Giraffes Fly And <u>Madly</u> Gather Five Eggs twice?*

However, in practice it's usually quite easy to recall which **chords** are altered (**minor, diminished, added 6th** etc.), so, unless it really helps to add another letter to the mnemonic (or a number in the case of an **added 6th** or a **7th**), just keep it as short as possible.

The sample song **verse** we have been looking at has a **chord change** on the first beat of every bar, as many songs do. But what about those songs (and there are lots of them) that don't follow such a straightforward rhythmic pattern? Songs can have more than one **chord** in a bar, and styles like **jazz**, **Latin-American** and **reggae** often have irregular or **syncopated rhythms** where **chord changes** occur on the up-beat.

With such songs it may be necessary to take some time to focus only on the **rhythm**, listening carefully to the **accompaniment** instruments whilst trying to ignore the singer. It can also be very helpful to tap or clap along with the **rhythm**, keeping in perfect time with the music, as you listen to the song. Becoming *physically* involved in the music like this (rather than just listening) can really help when you're trying to get the hang of tricky musical **rhythms**.

Whenever you are confident that you understand and can 'feel' a **rhythm** you can then apply it to the song's **chord** sequence (which you'll have worked on separately).

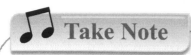

Take Note

LOL, it's an acronym!

Sometimes a **chord** progression is more easily remembered as a simple acronym. For example, the **chord** progression **D, A, D, G, A, G** has a certain flow as '*DAD-GAG*', or **C, Am, C, Am, G, Em** as *CAM-CAM-GEM* (where 'M' represents **minor** in the **Am** and **Em** chords).

Hidden words

Occasionally, part of a **chord** sequence will form a word, as in the example below.

| D | D | Em | Em A7 | D | Bm | G A | D |

| Bm E7 | A | D | G| D A7 | D | G A | Em |

Taking just the main letters of the first six **chords** in the opening five bars we get **DEAD**! We would have to remember that the **E** is **E minor** and the **A** is **A7**, but, as mentioned before, in practice these things are usually easier to recall than extended **chord** sequences. Besides, we are only using memory-joggers, not a mathematical system!

For the next four bars - **Bm, G, A, D** - we might find that a simple acronym, **BM-GAD**, works, or perhaps a mnemonic such as **B**ig **M**enacing **G**hosts **A**re **D**opey. That would reduce the first 8 bars to either **DEAD BM-GAD** or **DEAD B**ig **M**enacing **G**hosts **A**re **D**opey. And for the following 8 bars how about **BEAD, G**o **D**ad, **G**o **A**nd **E**at?

Crazy? Certainly. But hopefully pretty helpful, too. Here are two more:

| F | C | G7 | C | Bb| Gm | C7 | C | '**F**at **C**hickens **G**o **C**razy **B**efore **G**oing **C**ool & **C**alm'

| A7 | D | A | E| E7 | D | A | '**A**nd **7 D**ogs **A**te **E**ach **7 D**odgy **A**pples.'

It's a case of chronic mnemonic!

Choose a song containing between 6 and 10 different **chords** and commit it to memory using the techniques just described. Begin by outlining the main sections and looking for patterns and **repeats** that will reduce the total amount of original information that has to be memorised. Then, using mnemonics, acronyms and any other quirky little memory-joggers, reduce this down further as much as you can, ideally to just a couple of lines of information.

Keep experimenting with this method and you should be able to steadily increase your memorised song repertoire without suffering any headaches!

Part 3: Improvisation

Musical improvisation is a very natural and enjoyable way to express yourself and, although experienced musicians can make it look like a very complex skill that requires a special 'gift', it's not at all difficult to get impressive and reliable results every time, regardless of your experience, if you employ some simple techniques.

Improvisation can be used as part of any piece you play in your Higher Music performance exam, but it **CANNOT** be used for the whole piece.

Basic Improvising tutorial video

You may find it useful to watch the video '**Basic Improvising**' which explains some simple techniques for improvising easily but effectively over a backing track. The video is suitable for absolute beginners and those who would like to improvise smooth melodies reliably every time. You can access this video by clicking on the audio icon above (e-book) or on the jm-education YouTube channel at *www.youtube.com/jm-education*.

Some basic steps for easy and effective improvising

Note: this section refers to improvising on a musical instrument, but the same techniques can be used for improvised ('**scat**') singing.

1. Begin by choosing a **scale** you find easy to play. This can be a **major**, **minor** or **pentatonic scale**.

2. Next, rather than thinking about improvising, phrases or speed, just play some long, **sustained** notes from your chosen **scale** to create a series of notes that 'sing.' To help you achieve this, imagine how a singer performs long notes in a slow song. The notes will be **legato**, not **staccato**, and sound relaxed. Your goal is to achieve the same effect with your instrument, using good technique and listening carefully as you play.

Play over an instrumental backing track

3. Now it's time to select a backing track in the same **key** as your chosen **scale** - preferably one that isn't too fast or heavy. Including the key words 'chill out', 'ambient' or 'slow' in the URL search window will help you locate suitable tracks online.

4. Listen to your chosen backing track for at least a minute or two before attempting to improvise over it. This will allow you to become familiar with the beat and general **style** of the music, making it easier to keep in time with the track when you begin to play.

5. Now start playing your long, **sustained**, singing notes over the track and notice how you immediately get a nice result! That's because good improvising is not about playing lots of random notes but creating phrases that have shape - rather like a wordless song you are 'singing' with your instrument.

When you feel comfortable with these basic steps to 'instant improvising' in your chosen **key**, you can start to incorporate other elements into your playing, one at a time.

Taking it to the next level

Here are some things that will immediately make your improvising sound more accomplished:

- Use long and short note values to vary the **rhythm** and so create shape in your improvisation.

- Play in phrases. Don't just ramble on with passages of notes that have no shape. Think about the **rhythms** of speech and the average length of song phrases. The **rhythm** of song melodies varies naturally to suit the syllables in the lyrics and you can imitate such melodic phrases when you improvise.

- Just as singers have to breathe, so your solo improvisation should take a breath at regular intervals. This can be achieved simply by using a longer, **sustained** note at the end of a flowing passage of notes, or by inserting a **pause** or **rest**. This technique also produces natural musical phrases.

 **Take Note**

Cool cadences

You can create **cadences** at the end of your phrases using this simple method:

* To make a **perfect cadence**, end the phrase on the **key** note (e.g. in the **key** of **G major**, end on the note **G**)

* To make an **imperfect cadence**, end the phrase on any note EXCEPT the **key** note

- Depending on the **style** of the music, you might choose to play some **chromatic passing notes** to give your solo added melodic colour. A **chromatic passing note** can be created by playing the **chromatic** note (not found in the **scale**) between two notes which are a **tone** apart, thereby producing three **stepwise** notes played one after the other. For example: **C, C#, D**, where the **passing note** is of course **C#**; or **A, Bb, B**, where the **passing note** is **Bb**. All **passing notes**, by definition, must be played as part of a stepwise 3-note progression (either **ascending** or **descending**) where they function as a note that 'passes' from one note of the **scale** to another. **Chromatic passing notes** work especially well in **Jazz** and **Blues** music.

 Great advice... **Top Tip**

Speed kills

Don't try to play faster than your current technical ability allows. Awkward attempts at speed sound amateurish, whereas slower, **legato** phrases that make your instrument 'sing' will always sound more professional.

Even in a piece of music or backing track that has a fast **tempo/beat**, you don't have to play fast; as long as your notes follow the beat of the music you could play a **sustained** note on every second, fourth or eighth beat (or whatever), and your solo will still fit nicely.

Top Tip

Using backing tracks is like playing with a band whenever you want

Two more essential tips for playing effectively with backing tracks:

1. Be careful to listen to and follow the beat of the track as you play, ensuring you are always keeping time with the music. To make this easier, set the volume of the backing track to a level that can be heard clearly as you improvise.

2. When improvising well with a backing track the improvisation should flow and sound like a natural part of the track, as though it was composed especially for it, and the player is the extra band member that the music had been missing to make it complete!

Below is a list of some online sources that will be useful for locating backing tracks, songs and guitar tabs. Most of the backing tracks are of a professional standard, so, to develop your improvising skills, you only have to type your preference for **key** and musical **style** in the search bar and off you go!

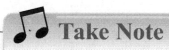

Take Note

Sites for song lyrics with chords, backing tracks and guitar tabs

- ** www.youtube.com Backing tracks in every **key** and a wide range of musical **styles**

- www.chordie.com An extensive library of songs in lyric/chord/tab format

- www.ultimate-guitar.com Despite the title, the huge song library in this site may be useful for all musicians, not just guitarists

- * www.yalp.io An interactive musical resource where you can play along with song videos or backing tracks while the **accompaniment chords** scroll on-screen as the track progresses

- * www.chordify.net An interactive resource with many features including play-along song videos and backing tracks

   * Both **yalp.io** and **chordify.net** allow you to change the **key** of the track and alter its playback speed to either slow down the music (for easier practising) or speed it up when you are ready to fly! They also have optional premium services where you can pay for additional musical resources. ** You can alter the playback speed of **YouTube** videos/backing tracks by clicking on the video 'settings' icon and adjusting 'playback speed.'

Group performing

Group performing can be a very enjoyable musical and social activity, involving a little less of the pressure associated with solo performing. However, certain skills and attitudes are required of each musician in a group if they, and the group as a whole, are to be successful.

For example, unlike solo performing where you only have to listen to your own playing, group performing involves listening to the overall sound of the whole group as you play, as well as your individual part in it. Becoming too absorbed in your own playing, or blocking out the other musicians, could mean that you don't notice when, for example, you're playing too loud or too quiet, or speeding up/slowing down within the group.

Each instrument/singer must contribute to the overall **timbre** and dynamic of the group. A self-indulgent electric guitarist or keyboard player who is playing too loud - or too much! - will drown out the singer and the balance will be ruined.

Here are some other important things that must be considered in group performing:

- Good **drums** and/or **bass guitar** are the 'backbone' of most bands as they generally set the **tempo** of the music (and therefore the regular **beat**) which every other band member will be following. So, **drum** and **bass** players need to have a good sense of **beat**, while the other performers must be able to follow that **beat** faithfully in every piece of music.

- **Be Committed**. To avoid problems, every member of the group should have a considerate and professional attitude, which means turning up for each rehearsal on time, practising their own parts beforehand until they are fluent, and always remembering that it is a *group*, not one performer with a huge ego accompanied by some other musicians who are only there to support!

- **Be patient** with other members of your group. Your responsibility is to work together as a team to make good music (and enjoy doing it), so bad tempers or uncooperative players will cause unnecessary difficulties that affect the quality of the music. Differences of opinion should be talked through, not argued over. Petty squabbles can easily destroy groups - something which has happened many times even among professional performers and famous groups - so try not to add to their number!

- **Rehearse regularly** and make sure every group member knows his/her responsibilities within the group.

 Take Note

Your individual attitude and behaviour within the group (not just your performing ability) will be taken into account for your final mark in the **Group performing** component of Higher Music.

How do I keep practice interesting if it's part of a regular routine?

Even though we may love playing a musical instrument or singing, there are times when the thought of having to practise regularly can be unappealing. So how can we keep it interesting?

- **Try starting your practice session by improvising to some online backing tracks.** Engaging in an undemanding and expressive musical activity like this will help to ease you into playing and quickly get you into the right frame of mind for more focused study - like exam pieces. Improvising has the added advantage of being an ideal way to warm up muscles or vocal cords.

- **Begin with music you can already play well.** Starting off a session by playing easy or more familiar music has two benefits: **1.** It is a good way to warm up. **2.** You'll be maintaining the standard of your musical repertoire, ensuring you don't lose any good work already done.

- **Mix up the bars.** Don't practise the same way each time. When you are learning to play a piece of music you don't need to start at the beginning - the end may be just as good a place to start!

- **Choose a good time.** Try to practise at a time of day when you are most alert and energy levels are high. If this isn't possible, at least have a short rest and a snack before beginning a practice session to refresh yourself physically and mentally.

Great advice...   **Top Tip**

Finding it hard to self-motivate? Try sneaking up on yourself

Self-discipline is a challenge for most of us, so if you are feeling a bit unmotivated, try some of these strategies:

- Sometimes the hardest thing about music practice is simply *starting.* So, if you can, leave your music out on the stand and (if appropriate) your instrument handy so that you don't have to first undergo a 'setting up' process before you can start playing. Students often comment that the hardest part of practice is motivating themselves to get their instrument out of the case!

- Don't let the thought of a 30 minute practice session put you off practising at all that day, but if you feel that you just can't face it, at least try to put in a small amount of time, since a short 'hit' of focused practise is much better than none.

- Remember that playing and listening to music can be relaxing, so don't think of practice sessions as one of your daily 'must do' activities so much as a pleasant escape from them!

Final preparation for the performance

- **Being prepared reduces stress**, so get your exam pieces performance-ready well before the exam. Bearing in mind that nerves can threaten to take the edge off a performance, you should be aiming to play your music at about 120 percent when practising in order to achieve 100 percent under pressure. As well as making sure your pieces are prepared for the performance, you should also allocate time to prepare both your equipment and yourself.

- **Ensure your instrument is in working order and good condition**. On a string instrument an old or inferior quality bow will produce a harsh tone and old strings reduce both volume and sound quality, whilst a poor reed can have the same effect on certain wind instruments. So, if strings or reed have to be replaced do this at least a few days before the exam to allow them to settle in and, in the case of strings, retain their pitch when they are tuned. If you will be singing, you may want to bring a small bottle of water or throat pastilles into the exam room.

- **Get others to listen**. When you feel your performance programme is ready for others to hear, ask your teacher or friends to listen to it as this will give you some essential practice in performing for people.

Great advice... **Top Tip**

Give yourself a break

Playing music isn't an exact science. We all make mistakes. Even world-class musicians can make performance errors for any number of reasons - memory slip, a moment's loss of concentration - as well as some they simply won't be able to account for.

It's normal to be disappointed with some of your performances when playing to an audience (even if it's just one person), or to feel that you've let yourself down because you haven't played as well as you know you can. But you must not be discouraged, because every time you play for other people you gain invaluable experience - even if it doesn't go especially well. Many musicians have commented that poor performances ultimately made them better players because they became so determined to overcome any issues that their performing abilities improved quicker!

It makes no sense, therefore, to become too disheartened by a weak performance. Instead, learn from it and use it as fuel for a renewed determination to improve. Used in this way, poor performances can become the foundation for success!

- **Performing has to be practised, too**. Playing live for people requires practice, just like the music itself, since you have to develop a certain ability to focus on playing without thinking about who's listening, or worrying about making mistakes. If at first you feel very self-conscious or nervous, try this: rather than getting people to sit down and listen attentively to you, just play while they are nearby, engaged in other tasks, but still able to hear you. This will take some of the pressure off whilst gradually helping you to become accustomed to playing for others.

- **Record yourself**. Making an audio or video recording allows you to privately watch and/or listen to yourself performing in order to consider what you may want to improve on. It will also help to simulate exam conditions as you'll probably feel under a bit of pressure, so use that situation to analyse the feeling and work on keeping your focus. You will now also appreciate how it really helps to have your music fluent, or memorised, when the pressure is on! And it's perfectly natural to cringe when you first hear or see yourself performing, but don't worry, you'll soon get over that!

- **Welcome feedback, disregard negative criticism**. Another option is to record and post your performance on social media. Getting some compliments or likes will help to boost your confidence, but it's very important not to become either big-headed with positive comments or upset by negative ones. Some people attack others because of ignorance, jealousy or just to get noticed, whereas wiser individuals offer constructive criticism - or say nothing at all!

- **Give careful consideration to the playing order of the pieces in your programme**. Don't just play your performance pieces in a random order; give some thought to how each one contributes to the overall programme. For example, playing two calm pieces followed by two dramatic ones may be less effective than alternating between calm and dramatic and thereby maintaining a sense of contrast that will likely be more engaging for the listener. Starting the programme with a piece you feel especially confident about playing is also a good idea (although, ideally, this should be all of them!), and certainly DO NOT make the mistake of playing the hardest one first just to 'get it out of the way.' On the contrary, try to leave more demanding music to a point in your performance when you will have settled down and be well into the flow of playing.

- **Find out where you can have a warm-up before going in to the performance exam**. Having some private preparation time to warm-up and settle before the performance is very important. If possible don't wait until the day of the exam to find out where you can do this since any unexpected late information or confusion will only create stress.

- **Is your accompanist also prepared?** If you will be using an accompanist, make sure you have at least a couple of practice sessions together so that you can both become familiar with performing as a duet and sort out any musical issues that may need attention.

- **Rest well**. Lack of proper rest affects concentration, mood and overall performance, so making sure you are getting enough sleep is an important part of the preparation process.

- **Eat well**. Good food assists concentration, helps keep you alert and your energy levels high. Junk food, on the other hand, can make you listless and irritable, and too much tea or coffee might make you feel tense or shaky, all of which will provoke feelings of stress.

Practise yourself performance fit

You wouldn't expect to become physically fit just because you know *how* to use all of the fitness machines in the gym. Music practice is the same. Simply knowing what's involved in a piece of music doesn't mean you will be able to play/sing it properly. Remember: regular practice is a necessary physical activity as well as an intellectual process which keeps the muscles or voice sufficiently conditioned to play or sing well.

Don't forget to practise making mistakes - or rather, how to handle them!

An error-free performance is of course something you should always be aiming for. However, mistakes do occur, especially under pressure, but they only become a problem if you react badly to them.

A mistake in one part of the music shouldn't affect your concentration so much that it causes you to falter in the next. You must NOT go back and 'fix' a mistake when you are performing live as this will only make it more obvious - and therefore bigger. Instead, carry on from the most convenient point in the music nearest to where things went wrong. The only exception to this would be if the mistake happens right at the very start of a piece; in which case you should stop, take a moment to compose yourself, and begin again.

You can practise dealing with mistakes simply by resuming the flow of the music as soon as possible every time you make an error in a piece of music, as opposed to stopping or returning to the beginning to start over.

Knowing *what to do* in the event of a mistake is good performance preparation, and it will give you a lot more confidence than simply hoping nothing goes wrong. If done well, it's even possible to cover up a performance error so effectively that only you (not the audience) notice it. I call this 'damage limitation' and it's something that all experienced musicians do if they make a slip during live performance.

The performance

Things the visiting examiner will be looking for in your performance

In your exam you are basically required to demonstrate your technical and musical ability through the accurate, flowing performance of each piece - as opposed to uncertain or erratic playing resulting from lack of proper preparation!

Listed below are the things the examiner will be listening to and giving you credit for, and you should therefore keep these in mind as you prepare for the performance.

Technical and musical elements the examiner will be considering

Tempo
Is the speed appropriate for the **style** of the piece and/or the composer's suggested **tempo** (e.g. **Lento**, **Andante**, **Allegro**)? Does it have continuity and flow?

Rhythm
Are the rhythms being played completely accurately in accordance with what is written in the music and/or stylistically appropriate?

Melody
Is the **melody** clear and flowing? Does it have an intonation (tone quality) that fits with the **style** and character of the piece?

Harmony
Are the **chords** and/or **bass** line being played accurately and clearly with no damped sounds or unclear notes within the **chord**? Is the **harmony** being played at a suitable volume without overpowering the **melody**?

Character
Is the character of the piece being interpreted convincingly? For example, a dance would be light with a confident and clearly defined beat; a love song would be performed with appropriate feeling in order to convey the emotions suggested by the lyrics and music.

Dynamics
Are the **dynamics** being performed with regard to what is on the printed music or appropriate to the **style** and mood of the music? Is there sufficient and accurate contrast between the various **dynamics**?

Tone
Is the tone clear and suitable for the music? Is it controlled, secure and pleasant to listen to or harsh and unsympathetic to the mood of the piece? Is the performer showing an understanding of how tone changes can be made - for example, on a stringed instrument by moving either closer to the bridge or further away from it; on piano by how hard or soft the keys are struck, or by the way the voice is used? Is mood and character being applied to the piece through an effective use of tone?

Mood
Does every aspect of the performer's playing help to convey the mood of the music accurately and sensitively? Is contrast also achieved between each piece in the programme through these aspects of musicianship?

Examiners are basically on your side

It must be stressed that the examiner will NOT be looking to criticise your playing or deduct marks every time you make a slip because of performance nerves. Their job is to credit every positive aspect of your playing rather than focus on the negative. That's why you should never dwell on any mistakes made during live performance, but instead continue playing as though nothing has happened and show what you can do.

It also has to be said that the examiner will usually be able to distinguish between mistakes that can happen to anyone during a live performance and those which are obviously the result of insufficient practice. So make sure you have prepared properly!

 Take Note

How you can impress by making a mistake

Examiners are likely to be impressed if you *cope well* after making a mistake because they know these four things:

1. You are probably nervous
2. Performing well to a live audience (even if only one person) often requires a lot of experience
3. Resuming the flow of the music after making a mistake shows a professional attitude
4. You are only human, so mistakes can happen.

Examiners are musicians themselves and understand perfectly well how you feel. They are also more experienced, which means they have already made a lot more mistakes than you!

So, if you make any mistakes during live performance, just remember to respond to them like a professional.

Other advice for the performing exam

- Make sure you know all the arrangements for the exam well in advance, such as time, place and any other relevant information. If you need an accompanist, ensure they are reliable and also know about the exam arrangements.

- Have a short warm-up before going in to the exam. This shouldn't be considered a final practice session but just a little time (10-20 minutes) devoted to preparing your voice or fingers/hands and getting you into the zone where your playing or singing starts to flow. Don't spend too long on this as you will risk taking the edge off your performance.

- Nervous tension can dry up your mouth and cause a feeling of lethargy, so stay hydrated. Drinking water at regular intervals will help you remain alert and focused and is especially important if you are going to be singing, so carry a bottle with you on performance day.

- Get to the exam room area as early as possible. Arriving in plenty of time allows you to become accustomed to the atmosphere and avoid unnecessary stress caused by rushing to get there - which will prevent you from focusing properly before the exam. The last thing you want after all your practice and preparation is to rush into the exam, out of breath and mentally unprepared. Get settled in and get into exam mode!

- Once you are in the exam room DO NOT RUSH TO START PLAYING as this might cause a false start where you make a mistake at the beginning of the opening piece and have to begin again. Get comfortable first. If you will be reading music set it on the stand carefully. If you are playing **piano** or **keyboard** make sure the chair or stool is set at a good height for you. Last of all, take a few moments to 'hear' the opening bars of the first piece inside your head before you start playing, just to make sure you begin at the correct **tempo**. (You should, in fact, do this before playing every piece in the programme.)

- Now that you have come this far and done all of the preparatory work it's time to put *yourself* into the music by playing with feeling and conviction. Don't worry about any mistakes you make, or those you *might* make; the examiner wants to hear the real, musical *you* coming through. So let go and put everything into it!

You already possess the greatest skill of all

Music notation and guitar tab are just graphic ways of representing note **pitches**, musical **rhythm** and **dynamics** etc., and if you simply follow these visual instructions without interpreting and *feeling* what the composer is trying to convey through those symbols then a machine may as well be performing!

Music is a form of human expression (some would say the highest form) and therefore performing it well requires a thinking, feeling human being with the ability - not just the technical capability - to pass on an emotional experience to others through the music. Only *you* can make music by bringing all the elements to life in your own unique way. And that is one of the most satisfying and enjoyable aspects of performing music; creating an experience - whether it's uplifting, joyful, motivating, transcendent, sad, angry, dramatic - ultimately through an incredible ability you already have waiting inside you. So don't forget to access it every time you perform!

Great advice... **Top Tip**

A final little piece of important advice...

When I had just started learning to play an instrument, a musician whose work I admire made a comment that inspired and stuck with me throughout my musical career...

'I would say a mark of a good musician is if you can play one note and mean it, it's better than being able to play zillions of scales and not mean it.' Mike Oldfield.

Of course he meant that genuine feeling and expression are more important than technical ability alone. With expression you can make even the simplest piece of music come alive. It doesn't have to be complex or fast to be impressive.

Being a musician, your powers of expression mean more than, say, the speed of your fingers! Communication is everything. If you feel something, it will be present in every note you play - and that's what will make people really listen to and enjoy your music.

Glossary of musical concepts

Higher STYLE Concepts

Chamber music – music intended to be played in a room (as opposed to a larger venue such as a concert hall or theatre) by a small **ensemble**. Chamber music typically consists of a few musicians (trios, quartets, quintets etc) with one player for each part, where each part is of equal importance in the group. The **string quartet** is perhaps the best example of a chamber music group.

Impressionist – a musical style, first appearing in the 1870's, where the expression of a mood (often dreamy and romantic) or an emotion is the most important aspect, and musical structure is looser. Other characteristics include **whole tone scales**, **rubato** and **chord** extensions such as 6ths, 9ths, major 7ths etc. which can be used to create more expansive, 'floating' or dreamy sounds. Impressionist composers include Debussy, Delius, Ravel and Satie.

Jazz-funk – a fusion of jazz, funk, soul and R&B music that began in America in the 1960's and continued developing in the 1970's with the use of analogue synthesizers and electric piano alongside instruments such as **bass guitar**, **drums**, **electric guitar**, **trumpet**, **trombone**, **saxophone** and **vocals**. Characteristic features include repetitive **riffs** (commonly referred to as 'grooves' in this style), improvisation, electronic sounds and sometimes **scat singing**. Musicians and bands associated with jazz-funk include Miles Davis, George Benson, Herbie Hancock, Kool and the Gang and Earth, Wind and Fire.

Lied (plural: *Lieder*) – German word for 'song', but it usually refers more particularly to art songs of the **romantic** era which were **accompanied** on **piano**. The songs (lieder) – which were often **strophic** with a **ternary** structure – focused on poetry, drama, scene-setting and character in an expressive way that was typical of the **romantic** period. Famous lieder composers include Schumann, Mendelssohn, Wagner, Strauss, Brahms, Wolf, Liszt and Schubert (who was widely recognised as one of the finest of all lieder composers.)

Mass – a large-scale religious vocal work based mainly on the Roman Catholic High Mass (which was sung). The mass is divided into two parts; the *Ordinary*, which contains the unchanging sections of the mass (the *Kyrie, Gloria, Credo, Sanctus Benedictus, Agnus Dei* and *Benedicamus Domino*), and the *Proper*, a musical setting (normally based on **plainchant**) of those parts of the mass which were varied depending on the occasion. Dating from the 7th century, the mass underwent various transformations over the centuries which were partly influenced by musical developments. The simple **chants** used in the earliest times became the basic melodic material on which later masses were composed, and from this came the use of **polyphony**. By the mid 15th century, melodies from non-religious *chansons* (songs) were also used as a source for the tenor part around which original melodies were composed. This practice of weaving existing material with new music was common, and masses could be based on *chansons, motets* or *madrigals* (types of song) written by late renaissance composers such as Palestrina and Morales.

In the **baroque** period composers divided the various sections of the mass into several musical movements and used either **choruses** with instrumental doubling, or **solo voices** and independent instrumental **accompaniment** - the *Mass in B minor* by J S Bach is perhaps the finest example of this style. Haydn and Mozart's masses of the **classical** period show the influence of the **symphony** in their style, and later masses by Beethoven (the *Missa Solemnis* mass in C), Liszt, Bruckner and Stravinsky were written for concerts or special occasions rather than religious services.

Musique concrète – an experimental technique in musical composition using recorded sounds as raw material. The term was first used in the late 1940's by early electronic composers in Paris to describe 'concrete' sounds which were recorded using analogue tape recorders rather than being written down as musical notation that had to be performed later. Instead of using musical instruments, the recorded sounds came from natural, everyday objects (anything from the sound of doors closing to car horns and squeaking chairs!) which were then arranged into a rhythmic sound composition. The technique is one of the earliest examples of electronic music and a precursor to computer-generated sounds and digital sampling.

Oratorio – a large work for **orchestra** (consisting of **ripieno** and **concertino** sections, each with its own **basso continuo**), **chorus** and **soloists**, based on a religious or moral text and normally set dramatically (like a play). In its earlier forms (around 1600-1650), scenery and costumes were also used (as in an opera), but these were discarded in later oratorios which were written for concert performance only. From the mid 17th century onwards the more developed oratorio was typically a work in two sections (which could last up to two hours in total), with many **Da Capo arias** and a few **choruses**. Famous oratorios come from the **baroque** and early **classical** periods, such as *Messiah* by Handel and *The Creation* and *The Seasons* by Haydn, but later composers also wrote oratorios, including Liszt (*Christus*), Elgar (*The Dream of Gerontius*) and Walton (*Belshazzar's Feast*). Although normally a religious work, some non-religious oratorios were also written, such as *Semele* by Handel and *A Child of our Time* by twentieth-century composer Michael Tippett.

Plainchant – a religious chant from the early Christian church, sung in Latin and commonly performed by men (usually monks) singing **modal, melismatic** phrases in **unison**. Also known as Gregorian chant or Plainsong.

Recitative – a form of speech-singing (half-spoken, half-sung) where the performer has some freedom with the **rhythm** (which closely follows the natural **rhythm** of speech); sometimes this freedom also extends to the notes and how they are sung. Used in works such as **opera** and **oratorio** as a lead-up to a song or a means of linking **arias**, but also as a device to inform the audience of a plot development and so move the drama along (this could be a dialogue between two characters, for example). Two main kinds of recitative are: **accompanied recitative** (which is accompanied by instruments, **continuo** or **orchestra**) and *dry* **recitative** - which was almost entirely **unaccompanied**, except for the occasional appearance of an instrument such as a **harpsichord** to punctuate certain of the speaker's words.

Sonata – a composition either for **solo piano**, or for a **solo** instrument with **piano accompaniment**. Popular in the **classical** period, sonatas usually consisted of 3 movements with the **tempo** structure: **1:** Fast **2:** Slow **3:** Fast. In the late **classical** and early **romantic** periods, sonatas became longer and an extra penultimate movement (a *minuet and trio (or scherzo)*) was added, making the structure: **1:** Fast **2:** Slow **3:** minuet and trio (or scherzo) **4:** Fast. * A minuet is a lively dance in **triple metre**, and the trio (or scherzo) its contrasting middle section.

Soul music – a style of popular music influenced by **gospel**, **blues**, **jazz** and country music developed by African-American musicians in the 1960's, where the performer displays strong and sincere emotions through a very expressive singing style.

String quartet – a **chamber music** ensemble - comprising two **violins**, a **viola** and a **cello** - that began in the **classical** period with Haydn and was developed by composers including Mozart and Beethoven who wrote string quartets in four movements using **sonata**, **rondo** and *minuet and trio* form. The style is still important today.

Higher MELODY/HARMONY Concepts

Acciacciatura – a note which is to be played as quickly as possible before the note it precedes. This is an **ornament**, written smaller than standard notes, with a line scored across it indicating that it has no time value and should be 'crushed in' very quickly:

Added 6th – a **chord** which has the **interval** a 6th higher than the root note added to it. For example, the **G major** triad consists of the notes, **G,B,D**, and the **interval** a 6th higher than **G** is **E**, so the notes of a **G added 6th chord (G6)** are **G,B,D,E**.

Diminished 7th (chord) – a **diminished chord** (a triad made up of **minor 3rd intervals**) with the **diminished 7th interval** added on top. For example, the notes of the **D diminished chord** are **D, F, Ab**, and with the added **diminished 7th interval** the notes are **D, F, Ab, Cb** (**D dim7**).

Diminished triad – a 3-note **chord** (triad) consisting of two **minor 3rd intervals**. For example, **G, Bb, Db** in the **chord** of **G diminished**. (**G-Bb** is a **minor 3rd interval**, as is **Bb-Db**.)

Dominant 7th (chord) – the **dominant chord** (**chord V**) with the 7th note of the *key scale* added on top. For example, in the **key** of **C major** the **dominant chord** (**chord V**) is **G major** (consisting of the notes **G,B,D**) and the 7th note of the **C major scale** is **F**, so the **dominant 7th chord** in the **key** of **C major** is **G7**, consisting of the notes **G, B, D, F**.

Harmonic minor scale – a version of the **minor scale** where the 7th note is raised by a **semitone** when the **scale** is both **ascending** and **descending**. For example, the notes of the **scale** of **A minor harmonic** are: (ascending); **A B C D E F G# A**, (descending); **A G# F E D C B A**.

Interval – the distance in **pitch** between two notes. For example, the **interval** between **C** and **E** is a **3rd** (**C,D,E**) because there are three notes described. The **interval** between **F** and **C** is therefore a **5th** (**F,G,A,B,C**) because five notes are described.

Interrupted cadence – a type of **imperfect cadence** where **chord V** (the **dominant chord**) is followed by **chord VI** (the *submediant* **chord**), to create a slightly unexpected change of direction (or a little surprise) in the **harmony**, since the 'expected' **chord I** (which would complete a **V-I perfect cadence**) is replaced by **chord VI** (a **minor chord**) and so has 'interrupted' the anticipated **perfect cadence**.

Melodic minor scale – a version of the **minor scale** where the 6th and 7th notes are raised by a **semitone** when the **scale** is **ascending**, but lowered again by one **semitone** when the **scale descends**. For example, the notes of the **scale** of **A minor melodic** are: (ascending); **A B C D E F# G# A**, (descending); **A G F E D C B A**.

Mode / modal – a type of **scale** used mainly in early music (the medieval and renaissance periods) before tonal music (music with a **key**) was developed - although **modal** music is still in use today, especially in **folk**, **rock** and some ethnic styles. The seven basic modes are called *Ionian, Dorian, Phrygian, Lydian, Mixolydian, Aeolean* and *Locrian*, and in their simplest form correspond to the notes **C, D, E, F, G, A** and **B** respectively. For example, if you begin on the note **D** on a **keyboard** instrument and play only the successive *white* keys for an **octave**, this is the *Dorian* **mode**. Do the same on the note **F** and you will play the notes of the *Lydian* **mode**. The specific order of **tones** and **semitones** (no black keys are used) give each **mode** its unique sound. For further information, see the *Composing Workshop*, Chapter 4, page 57.

Mordent – an **ornament** consisting of a rapid playing of the written note and the note a step above (or below), followed by the written note again. A **mordent** is indicated by the symbol: ᴧᴧ

Obbligato (instrumental) – an essential ('obligatory') part which, although less prominent in a piece of music, is nevertheless essential and must not be omitted from the performance. For example, the *obbligato horn solo* in the third movement of Mahler's fifth symphony.

Plagal cadence – a **cadence** where **chord IV** (the **subdominant chord**) is followed by **chord I** (the **tonic chord**). Sometimes called an 'Amen' **cadence** because it is often used at the end of hymns on the word 'Amen'.

Relative major/minor – every musical **key signature** has both a **major key** and a **minor key** associated with it. For example, the **key signature** with one **sharp** (**F#**) is shared by the keys of **G major** and **E minor**. Therefore, **E minor** is known as the **relative minor key** of **G major**, and **G major** as the **relative major key** of **E minor**.

Tierce de Picardie – a technique commonly used in the renaissance and **baroque** periods where a piece of music in a **minor key** ends on the **major chord**. For example, a piece in the **key** of **E minor** would finish with an **E major chord**.

Higher RHYTHM/TEMPO Concepts

3 against 2 – a **cross rhythm** where a **triplet rhythm** (involving three notes) plays at the same time as two notes which 'add up' to the same value. For example, three **crotchet triplet beats** playing against two **crotchet beats**.

Augmentation – where a passage of music is repeated in longer note values than when it was first played. For example, a section of music first played in **quavers** is repeated in **crotchets**.

Diminution – where a passage of music is repeated in shorter note values than when it was first played. For example, a section of music first played in **crotchets** is repeated in **quavers**.

Irregular time signatures – when the music does not fall into equal - or 'even' - beat groupings. For example, **5/8**, **7/8**, **7/4** and **5/4** time.

Time changes – when the **time signature** changes (any number of times) in a piece of music.

Triplets - a group of three notes of equal duration played in the time value of (usually) a single beat. For example, a group of three **quaver triplets** would be played in the time of one **crotchet beat**. Triplets are basically a portion of musical time that is divided into three equal parts.

Higher TEXTURE/STRUCTURE/FORM Concepts

Basso Continuo – often abbreviated to 'continuo', this is a term for the instrument or instruments responsible for establishing the **harmony** in a piece of (mainly) **baroque** music. The basso continuo can consist of a single instrument such as **organ** (normally used for sacred music), **harpsichord** or *lute* (for smaller ensembles), or, where a more **contrapuntal** texture is required in the **bass** part, a **cello**, **bassoon** or *bass viol*. However, more than one instrument is often used for the basso continuo, especially in larger-scale works like the **concerto grosso** (see page 129), and in a late **baroque concerto** different continuo instruments would be used for the **ripieno** and **concertino** sections of the orchestra (see entries for **ripieno** and **concertino**). As the main role of the basso continuo was to support the **melody** by providing **harmony** and a **bass** line, it was gradually replaced in the **classical** period when composers wrote all the required **harmony** notes into the music itself, but the basso continuo was still used in certain compositions.

Concerto grosso – a kind of **baroque concerto** comprising a **concertino** (small group of instruments) and the **ripieno** (larger, main group of instruments). The purpose of having two groups was mainly so that they could provide contrast with each other.

Da Capo aria – an aria in **ternary form** (ABA) where the instruction '***Da Capo***' (go back to the beginning) is given at the end of the B section, as opposed to the A section being written out again.

Exposition – the opening section of a movement in **sonata form** - or in a **fugue** - in which we first hear the theme (or group of themes) that will later be repeated/developed in the piece.

Passacaglia – a musical form, usually in slow **triple metre**, based on variations of a **melody** played over a **ground bass**. Composers of passacaglias include Monteverdi, Lully, Bach and Purcell.

Ritornello – a term used mainly in **baroque** music to describe a brief passage which returns frequently in a piece of music. Normally played by the **ripieno** and alternating with the soloist(s) in a **concerto grosso** or **aria**.

Sonata form – the most important structure for instrumental music from the **classical** period to the twentieth century. The form has three main sections: **1:** the first section, the *exposition*, 'exposes' the main musical material, which consists of *themes* divided into *first subject* (in the **tonic key**) and *second subject* (normally in either the **dominant key** or **relative major key**), both of which are separated by a *transition* passage and concluded by a *codetta* (brief **Coda**). **2:** the second section, the *development*, 'develops' the material of the *exposition* by *repeating* it with *variation* and in several different keys, ending in the **tonic key** in preparation for the next section. **3:** the final section, the *recapitulation*, 'recaps' the themes used in the *exposition* (perhaps with some **key changes**), normally in the same order, but with the *second subject* now in the **tonic key**. Sometimes an *Introduction* and a **Coda** are added to this basic sonata structure.

Subject – a main melodic idea in a composition (normally a **fugue**), but also used to describe a theme in the *exposition* section of a piece in **sonata form**.

Through-composed – a term used to describe either a vocal/choral composition in which there is little or no repetition (e.g. **verses** and **chorus**), or a piece of music with no definite form.

Higher TIMBRE/DYNAMICS Concepts

Coloratura – a term used in vocal music to describe sections decorated (by the singer) with elaborate flourishes of notes or musical **ornaments**. The technique requires considerable skill of the singer (normally a **soprano**), and good examples can be found in some of Mozart's operas.

Concertino – the **solo** group in a **baroque concerto** or **concerto grosso**.

Harmonics – notes of a particularly resonant sound quality with a clarity and sustain that cannot be achieved in normal playing. They can be produced on wind instruments by altering lip pressure or (in the case of **woodwind** instruments) by opening a nodal hole in the instrument. String instruments can produce 'natural' harmonics by lightly touching strings at specific points (over a **guitar** fret, for example) before playing them, and 'artificial' harmonics by holding down the string (as in normal playing) and bowing/plucking it either a **4th** or an **octave** (**interval**) higher, depending on the type of string instrument.

Ripieno – the larger group of players in a **baroque orchestra**, as distinct from the **concertino** (**solo** group), especially in the **concerto grosso**.

String quartet – a **chamber music** ensemble comprising two **violins**, one **viola** and one **cello**.

Tremolando / tremolo – the very rapid repetition of a note to create a trembling effect.

National 5 Concepts

Musical concept examples and instructional videos for every concept at National 5, 4 and 3 levels can be found on the *Resources* page of the jm-education website: **www.jm-education.com**.

National 5 RHYTHM/TEMPO Concepts
Rubato
Ritardando
Moderato
Cross rhythms
Compound time 6   9   12 8   8   8

National 5 TEXTURE/STRUCTURE/ FORM Concepts
Strophic
Binary A/B
Rondo ABACA - episode
Alberti bass
Walking bass
Ground bass
Homophonic
Polyphonic
Contrapuntal
Coda

National 5 MELODY/HARMONY Concepts
Atonal music
Atonal
Cluster chord
Chord progression (I, IV, V, VI in major keys)
Perfect cadence
Imperfect cadence
Inverted pedal
Chromatic scale
Whole tone scale
Grace note
Glissando
Modulation
Contrary motion
Trill
Syllabic
Melismatic
Countermelody
Descant (voice)
Pitch bend
Semitone
Tone

National 5 TIMBRE/DYNAMICS Concepts
Piccolo, oboe, bassoon
French horn, tuba
Viola
Castanets, hi-hat cymbals, bongo drums
Clarsach, bodhran
Sitar, tabla
Arco, pizzicato
Con sordino
Flutter-tonguing
Rolls
Reverb
Mezzo-soprano, baritone
A cappella

National 5 STYLE Concepts
Symphony
Gospel
Classical
Pibroch
Celtic rock
Bothy ballad
Waulking song
Gaelic psalm
Aria
Chorus
Minimalist
Indian

National 5 Literacy
Tones, semitones, accidentals (sharps, flats and naturals)
Scales, chords and key signatures of C major, G major, F major and A minor.
Leaps (in musical notes)
Dotted rhythms, dotted crotchet, dotted quaver
Scotch snap,   1st and 2nd time bars
ff - fortissimo,   *pp* - pianissimo,   *sfz* - sforzando

National 4 Concepts

National 4 STYLE Concepts	National 4 TIMBRE Concepts	National 4 MELODY/HARMONY Concepts	National 4 RHYTHM/TEMPO Concepts
Baroque	Brass band, wind band	Major/minor (tonality)	Syncopation
Ragtime	Violin, cello, double bass, harp	Drone	Scotch snap
Romantic	Flute, clarinet, saxophone, pan pipes, recorder	Broken chord/arpeggio	Strathspey
Swing		Chord progressions - chords I, IV and V (major keys)	Jig
Concerto	Trumpet, trombone		Simple time 2 3 4
Opera	Timpani, snare drum, bass drum, cymbals, triangle, tambourine, guiro, xylophone, glockenspiel	Change of key	4 4 4
Scots ballad		Pedal	Compound time
Mouth music	Harpsichord	Scale	Anacrusis
Reggae	Bass guitar	Pentatonic scale	Andante
African music	Distortion	Octave	Accelerando
Rapping	Muted	Vamp	Rallentando
	Soprano, alto, tenor, bass	Scat singing	A tempo
	Backing vocals	Ornament	Dotted rhythms

National 4 TEXTURE/STRUCTURE/FORM Concepts	
Canon	Theme and variation
Ternary /ABA	Cadenza
Verse and chorus	Imitation
Middle 8	

National 4 Literacy
Treble clef stave, C-A' range of notes from middle C to first ledger line A
Sequences,   repeat signs
Quaver, paired quavers, semiquaver, grouped semiquavers
mf - mezzo forte,   *mp* - mezzo piano

National 3 Concepts

National 3 STYLE Concepts	National 3 MELODY/HARMONY Concepts		National 3 RHYTHM/TEMPO Concepts	National 3 TEXTURE/STRUCTURE/ FORM Concepts
Blues	Ascending	Question and answer	Accent/accented	Unison/octave
Jazz			Beat/pulse	Harmony/chord
Rock	Descending	Improvisation	2, 3 or 4 beats in the bar	Solo
Pop	Step (stepwise)	Chord		Accompanied/ Unaccompanied
Rock 'n' roll	Leap (leaping)	Discord	On the beat/off the beat	
Musical	Repetition	Chord change	Repetition	Repetition
Scottish	Sequence		Slower/faster	Ostinato/riff
Latin-American			Pause	Round

National 3 TIMBRE Concepts	
Striking (hitting), blowing, bowing, strumming, plucking	Steel band
Orchestra, strings, brass, woodwind and percussion (tuned and untuned)	Scottish dance band
Accordion, fiddle, bagpipes	Folk group
Acoustic guitar, electric guitar	Voice
Piano, organ	Choir
Drum kit	Staccato, legato

National 3 RHYTHM/TEMPO (cont.)
March
Waltz
Drum fill
Adagio
Allegro

National 3 Literacy
Lines and spaces of the treble clef
Steps (in musical notes)
Repetition
Semibreve, dotted minim, minim, crotchet
Bar lines, double bar lines
f - forte, *p* - piano, cresc. - crescendo, dim. - diminuendo

131

Answers to exercises	**Chapter 1**

Unit 1. Higher Music STYLE concepts and general National 5 concepts listening exercises

Question 1. (a) Soul music (b) 3/4 Time or Triple metre (c) Piano

Question 2. (a) Mass (b) 4/4 Time or Common time or Quadruple metre (c) Polyphonic or Melismatic

Question 3. (a) Impressionist (b) Rubato (c) Woodwind

Question 4. (a) Chamber music (b) Instrument 1. Piano Instrument 2. Violin   Instrument 3. Cello
(Instruments can be listed in any order)

Question 5. (a) Recitative (b) Soprano (c) Harpsichord

Question 6. (a) Plainchant (b) ☑ Homophonic   ☑ Melismatic

Question 7. (a) Sonata   (b) ☑ Atonal   ☑ Cluster chord

Question 8. (a) Oratorio   (b) ☑ Homophonic   ☑ Timpani

Question 9. (a) Musique concrète

Question 10. (a) String quartet (b) ☑ Accelerando   ☑ Pizzicato

Question 11. (a) Jazz-funk   (b) ☑ Backing vocals ☑ Riff

Unit 2. Higher Music MELODY/HARMONY concepts and general National 5 concepts listening exercises

Question 1. Sequence, Staccato, Obbligato organ, Baroque

Question 2. (a) Mode/modal, A cappella, Strophic, 2. (b) Bodhran

Question 3. Pedal, Mordent, Perfect cadence, Pause

Question 4. 1. Acciaccatura 2. Triangle, Cymbals, Timpani 3. Ritardando or Rallentando 4. Triple 5. Romantic

Question 5. (a) Polyphonic, Melismatic, Tierce de Picardie 5. (b) Melodic minor scale

Question 6. Triple metre, Relative major/minor, Classical guitar

Question 7. Riff, Electric guitar, Distortion, Harmonic minor

Question 8. (a) ☑ Dominant 7th   8. (b) ☑ Added 6th   8. (c) ☑ Diminished 7th

Question 9. (a) ☑ Plagal cadence   9. (b) ☑ Interrupted cadence   9. (c) ☑ Perfect cadence

Unit 3. Higher Music RHYTHM/TEMPO concepts and general National 5 concepts listening exercises

Question 1. Bass guitar, Keyboard, Staccato, Time changes

Question 2. Fugue, Augmentation, Harpsichord, Trill

Question 3. 3 against 2, Key change, Riff

Question 4. Tempo change, Pizzicato, Irregular Time signatures, Imitation

Question 5. 1. Violin 2. Arco 3. Harpsichord 4. Quadruple metre (or 4/4 time/Common time) 5. Diminution

Chapter 1 (contd.)

Unit 4. Higher Music TEXTURE/STRUCTURE/FORM concepts
and general National 5 concepts listening exercises

Question 1. Sonata form, Subject, Exposition, Modulation

Question 2. Oboe solo, Sforzando (*sfz*), Imperfect cadence

Question 3. Countermelody, Ground bass, Passacaglia, 4/4 time (quadruple metre)

Question 4. Soprano, Ritornello, Trill, Basso continuo

Question 5. Perfect cadence, Key change, Ritardando, Da Capo aria

Question 6. Concerto grosso, Metre change, Imitation, Basso continuo

Question 7. Tenor voice, Key change, Through-composed

Unit 5. Higher Music TIMBRE/DYNAMICS concepts
and general National 5 concepts listening exercises

Question 1. Ripieno, Trill, Tempo change, Concertino

Question 2. Legato, Crescendo, Timpani roll, Tremolando/tremolo

Question 3. 1. ☑ Soprano   2. Coloratura   3. Opera   4. Aria   5. Perfect cadence

Question 4. Bass guitar, Harmonics, Pitch bends

Question 5. Modulation,   String quartet, Vibrato,   Staccato

Chapter 2 Music literacy

Activity interval exercise, p. 35.   5th, 3rd, 2nd, 6th, 4th, octave, 7th, 2nd, 5th, 7th, 4th, 3rd

Literacy Exercise 1

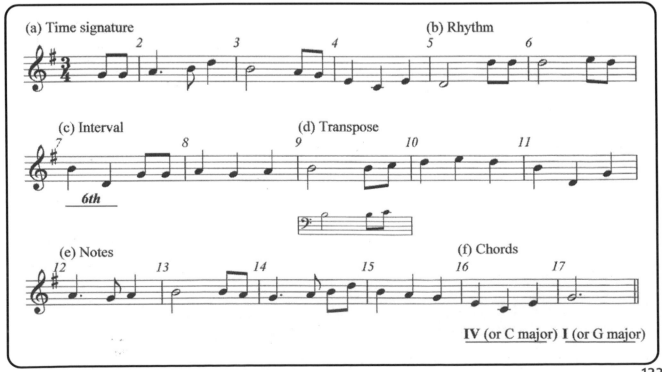

Chapter 2 (Contd.)

Literacy Exercise 2

Chapter 3 Specimen question paper

Question 1. (a) Inverted pedal, Mordent, Sonata   (b) Coloratura

Question 2. 1 The melody features an ascending *major* scale.

2 The playing technique used by the orchestral strings here is *pizzicato*.

3 The instrument playing the melody is a *classical guitar*.

4 The ornament here is a *trill*.

5 The style of this type of instrumental work is known as a *concerto*.

Question 3. (a) Impressionist   (b) 6/8 time or compound duple   (c) Jazz-funk

Question 4.

(b) Diminished 7th   (c) ✓ Augmentation

Question 6. Any **2** of these listed concepts from **each** of the three categories are acceptable answers:

Melody / Harmony	*Key Change, Trill, Perfect cadence, Repetition, Imperfect cadence, Contrary motion, Modulation*: *(major key - minor key - major key)*
Rhythm (Texture) / Tempo	*Triple metre, Basso continuo, Concerto grosso, Allegro, Ritornello*
Timbre / Dynamics	*Strings, Concertino, Ripieno, Arco, Slurs* *mf* (or *f*) - *mp* (or *p*) *(observations about dynamics count as* **one** *concept identified)*

Question 7.

Concepts		Column A Excerpt 1	Column B Excerpt 2	Column C 5 features common to both
Melody/Harmony	Ascending major scale			✓
	Interrupted cadence			
	Glissando			
	Key change			✓
Timbre	Harmonics			
	Woodwind solo			✓
	Timpani			✓
Texture/Structure/ Form	Rondo			
	Through-composed			
	Theme and variation			
Style	Impressionist			
	Symphony			✓
	Concerto			
				5 marks

Question 8.

Shine on, through the dark, shine on	1
Shine on, shine on...	2 *Syncopated*
We all pass through this world of changes	3 *Chords*
In a blink of forever's eye	4
But on the path of wisdom	5
We learn that nothing ever really dies	6 *Crescendo*
Shine on, in a new life, shine on	7 *Key*
Shine on, perfect star, shine on	8
Shine on, share the light, shine on	9
Shine on, shine on, shine on	10 *Unison*
Shine on, share the light	11
Shine on, always bright, shine on	12

Printed in Great Britain
by Amazon

19285076R00086